SUSTAINABLE FINANCE FOR ASIA AND THE PACIFIC
PROTECTING AND RESTORING CORAL REEFS

Martha Rogers, Carolina Rosales, Eric Roberts, and Fernando Secaira Fajardo

DECEMBER 2023

Creative Commons Attribution 3.0 IGO license (CC BY 3.0 IGO)

© 2023 Asian Development Bank
6 ADB Avenue, Mandaluyong City, 1550 Metro Manila, Philippines
Tel +63 2 8632 4444; Fax +63 2 8636 2444
www.adb.org

Some rights reserved. Published in 2023.

ISBN 978-92-9270-541-1 (print); 978-92-9270-542-8 (electronic); 978-92-9270-543-5 (ebook)
Publication Stock No. TCS230596-2
DOI: http://dx.doi.org/10.22617/TCS230596-2

The views expressed in this publication are those of the authors and do not necessarily reflect the views and policies of the Asian Development Bank (ADB) or its Board of Governors or the governments they represent.

ADB does not guarantee the accuracy of the data included in this publication and accepts no responsibility for any consequence of their use. The mention of specific companies or products of manufacturers does not imply that they are endorsed or recommended by ADB in preference to others of a similar nature that are not mentioned.

By making any designation of or reference to a particular territory or geographic area, or by using the term "country" in this publication, ADB does not intend to make any judgments as to the legal or other status of any territory or area.

This publication is available under the Creative Commons Attribution 3.0 IGO license (CC BY 3.0 IGO) https://creativecommons.org/licenses/by/3.0/igo/. By using the content of this publication, you agree to be bound by the terms of this license. For attribution, translations, adaptations, and permissions, please read the provisions and terms of use at https://www.adb.org/terms-use#openaccess.

This CC license does not apply to non-ADB copyright materials in this publication. If the material is attributed to another source, please contact the copyright owner or publisher of that source for permission to reproduce it. ADB cannot be held liable for any claims that arise as a result of your use of the material.

Please contact pubsmarketing@adb.org if you have questions or comments with respect to content, or if you wish to obtain copyright permission for your intended use that does not fall within these terms, or for permission to use the ADB logo.

Corrigenda to ADB publications may be found at http://www.adb.org/publications/corrigenda.

Notes:
In this publication, "$" refers to United States dollars, unless otherwise specified.
ADB recognizes "China" as the "People's Republic of China."

On the cover: **Tropics optics.** Anthias and their coral, part of the splendor of Verde Island, Philippines (photo by Andrew Delano from the TNC Photo Contest 2019).

CONTENTS

TABLES, FIGURES, AND BOXES v

FOREWORD vii

ACKNOWLEDGMENTS viii

ABBREVIATIONS ix

EXECUTIVE SUMMARY x

I   INTRODUCTION 1

II   BENEFITS OF CORAL REEFS 3

III   RISKS FACED BY CORAL REEFS AND THEIR IMPACTS 7
    A. Risks Coral Reefs Face in Asia and the Pacific 10
    B. Economic Returns of Healthy Coral Reefs in Asia and the Pacific 12

IV   ADDRESSING CORAL REEF DAMAGE 13
    A. Asexual and Sexual Propagation 13
    B. Physical Reef Restoration 16
    C. Artificial Reef Creation 17
    D. Emergency Restoration 19

V   INNOVATIVE FINANCING FOR MANAGING RISKS TO CORAL REEFS ... 21
    A. Parametric Insurance 22
    B. Other Innovative Financing Instruments 26

VI   A POST-DAMAGE RESPONSE MECHANISM TO IMPLEMENT 31
    AN EFFECTIVE FINANCIAL SCHEME
    A. Post-Damage Response Mechanism 32
    B. Institutional Arrangement to Buy and Manage a Coral Reef Insurance Policy ... 33
    C. Example: Parametric Insurance Policy in Quintano Roo, Mexico 34
    D. Example: Parametric Insurance Policy in Mesoamerican Reef 35

VII	**IDENTIFYING OPPORTUNITIES FOR CORAL REEF INSURANCE IN ASIA AND THE PACIFIC**	**37**
	A. Site-Specific Opportunities in Indonesia, the Philippines, Solomon Islands, and Fiji	40
	B. Broader Opportunities across Asia and the Pacific	49
VIII	**EXPANDING TO OTHER COASTAL ECOSYSTEMS**	**52**
	A. Mangroves	52
	B. Salt Marshes	54
	C. Oysters	55
	D. Sand Dunes	56
IX	**CONCLUSION**	**57**
	REFERENCES	**61**

TABLES, FIGURES, AND BOXES

TABLES

1	Description of Subset of Acute Stressors Faced by Coral Reefs Globally	8
2	Description of Chronic Stressor Faced by Coral Reefs Globally	9
3	Value of Economic Returns from Asia and the Pacific, Estimated 2030 and Annualized 2017–2030	12
4	Benefits and Limitations of Asexual and Sexual Propagation Methods	14
5	Commonly Used Physical Structures	18
6	Traditional Funding Sources Supporting Reef Restoration and Repair	21
7	Types of Parametric Insurance Structures for Coral Reefs	24
8	Innovative Funding Sources for Reef Management, Restoration, and Repair	30
9	Key Components of Post-Storm Response Mechanism	32
10	Institutional Arrangements to Implement Coral Reef Insurance Policy	33
11	Governance Structure in Mexico, Belize, Honduras, and Guatemala	36
12	Key Components of an Insurance Scheme for Post-Storm Response	37
13	Key Characteristics of Seven Potential Sites for an Insurance Policy in Indonesia	42
14	Key Characteristics of Seven Potential Sites for an Insurance Policy in the Philippines	44
15	Key Characteristics of Potential Site for an Insurance Policy in Solomon Islands	46
16	Key Characteristics of Potential Sites for an Insurance Policy in Fiji	48

FIGURES

1	Coral Reef Cover across Asia and the Pacific	1
2	Coral Reef Tourism Value across Asia and the Pacific	5
3	Coral Reef Provides Valuable Coastal Protection	6
4	Global Risks to Coral Reefs by Mean Annual Change and Extent of Damage	7
5	Tropical Storms and Cyclones in Asia and the Pacific (2010–2018)	11
6	Current and In-Development Reef Restoration Interventions	20
7	Components of Parametric Insurance Policy for Mesoamerican Reef Site	25
8	Structure of Trust Fund Managing Reef Insurance in Quintana Roo, Mexico	34
9	Potential Coral Reef Insurance Sites in Indonesia	40
10	Potential Coral Reef Insurance Sites in the Philippines	43

11	Potential Coral Reef Insurance Sites in Solomon Islands	46
12	Potential Coral Reef Insurance Sites in Fiji	48
13	Annual Expected People Protected from Flooding by Coral Reef across Asia and the Pacific	50
14	Social and Economic Dependence on Coral Reefs Overlaid with Integrated Local and Global Threats to Coral Reefs in 2030 and Typhoon Events, 2015–2018, in Select Regions of Asia and the Pacific	50
15	Mangrove Forest Cover across Asia and the Pacific	53
16	Salt Marsh Cover across Asia and the Pacific	55
17	Managing Risk Requires Different Financial Instruments	59
18	Process to Assess, Design, and Buy an Insurance Policy	59

BOXES

1	Gender Differences in Coral Reef Dependence	4
2	Typhoon Yolanda in the Philippines	11
3	Reef Restoration in the Philippines	15
4	Substrate Stabilization from Reef Recovery from Blast Fishing in Komodo National Park, 1998–2008	17
5	Mars Assisted Reef Restoration System	19
6	Parametric Insurance Policy in Quintana Roo, Mexico	23
7	Emergency Fund for the Mesoamerican Reef Fund	28
8	Feasibility of Mangrove Insurance in Gulf of Mexico and Caribbean	53

FOREWORD

Oceans cover over two-thirds of the surface of Earth. Yet, coral reefs, which occur in less than 1% of the ocean, support roughly one-quarter of all marine species. In the last 30 years, nonetheless, scientists estimate that we have lost over 50% of coral reefs and, currently, roughly 75% of the world's remaining coral reefs are threatened. The situation in Asia and the Pacific is more dire, with over 85% of remaining coral reefs threatened.

At the same time, as global population tops 8 billion, demand for food, energy, and water is growing rapidly, raising pressure on the oceans and their coral reefs. Meanwhile, climate change is heating up the oceans, intensifying storms, and causing more floods.

With over 150 million people living on or near coral reefs in Asia and the Pacific, the cumulative effect of coral reef loss, population growth, and climate change are affecting food, livelihoods, and safety. Coral reefs provide critical ecosystem services to these communities including protein, income, and shoreline protection from erosion by, for example, dissipating wave energy in storms. To restore ocean health and sustain the employment and sustenance we gain from the sea, immediate action is needed to protect towns and cities along coastlines, protect coastal livelihoods, and lower the risks emerging out of climate change.

The Asian Development Bank (ADB) and The Nature Conservancy (TNC) are focused on identifying innovative ways to effectively protect and restore critical ecosystems, such as coral reefs, in Asia and the Pacific. The need for funding and capacity to protect and restore coral reefs is too great to fill from any one source. The solution will require creative thinking and need to be multifaceted and diverse. The urgency of the crisis is too great to not invest now in identifying and developing innovative financial tools.

This report aims to increase momentum and awareness of the vast suite of potential opportunities to fund the much-needed protection and restoration of coral reef ecosystems in Asia and the Pacific. The collaboration between ADB and the TNC forms one aspect of their partnership since 2021, which rests on a shared commitment to advance nature-positive investment, environmental sustainability, and action on climate change across this unique region.

Ramesh Subramaniam
Director General and Group Chief
Sectors Group
Asian Development Bank

Will McGoldrick
Regional Managing Director
Asia Pacific
The Nature Conservancy

ACKNOWLEDGMENTS

The Asian Development Bank (ADB) prepared this report jointly with The Nature Conservancy (TNC), under the guidance of Thomas Kessler, principal finance specialist (Disaster Insurance), Finance, Sectors Group, ADB; with valuable and continuous directional advice throughout the process of Junkyu Lee, director, Finance, Sectors Group, ADB; and with the strong support of Ramesh Subramaniam, director general and group chief, Sectors Group, ADB; Bruno Carrasco, director general, Climate Change and Sustainable Development Department, ADB; Christine Engstrom, senior director, Finance, Sectors Group, ADB; Qingfeng Zhang, senior director, Agriculture, Food, Nature, and Rural Development, ADB; Arunkumar Samuel Abraham, senior environment specialist (ADB GEF consultant), Climate Change and Sustainable Development Department, ADB; Brigitte Balthasar, senior disaster and climate risk financing specialist, Climate Change and Sustainable Development Department; Melody Ovenden, senior social development specialist (Resettlement), Office of Safeguards, ADB; and Alessio Giardino, senior water specialist (Climate Change), Climate Change and Sustainable Development Department, ADB.

The TNC team was led by Martha Rogers, senior economist, TNC, and supported by Fernando Secaira, coastal risk and resilience lead, TNC; Carolina Rosales, coastal resilience Mexico assistant, TNC; and Eric Roberts, climate risk and resilience senior manager, TNC.

Throughout conception and drafting of the report, we received invaluable ideas, feedback, and comments from many individuals. We are grateful for the assistance and expert guidance provided by Daniel Morchain, global climate adaptation director, TNC; Jen Molnar, managing director/lead scientist policy and market analytics, TNC; Lizzie McLeod, global oceans director, TNC; Boze Hancock, senior marine restoration scientist, TNC; Jacob Davis, senior director sustainable finance, TNC; Laura Whitford, conservation partnerships director, TNC; Mark Way, head sustainability underwriting, Zurich North America; Simon Young, senior director, Willis Towers Watson (WTW); Sarah Conway, director, WTW; Jamie Pollard, associate director, WTW; Constance Wong, lead associate, WTW; and Josh Ling, disaster risk financing specialist, Global Shield Solutions Platform.

ABBREVIATIONS

ADB	Asian Development Bank
MAR Fund	Mesoamerican Reef Fund
SMEs	small and medium-sized enterprises
TNC	The Nature Conservancy
UN	United Nations
WTW	Willis Towers Watson
YKAN	Yayasan Konservasi Alam Nustantara (Indonesia)

EXECUTIVE SUMMARY

Coral reefs, located in more than 100 countries, are a critically important ecosystem (Asner et al. 2020). They support the broader health of coastal ecosystems and provide important services to nearby communities. In Asia and the Pacific, nearly 150 million people live within 30 kilometers of a coral reef and over half of coral reef fishers (3.8 million people) globally reside in the region (Burke et al. 2011a, Tey et al. 2013). One square kilometer of healthy coral reef can provide up to $900,000 in associated tourism value (Spalding et al. 2017). And coral reefs can dissipate wave energy, such as from tropical storms or swell waves, by as much as 97% (Ferrario et al. 2014). This reduces erosion and flooding and prevents damage to inland infrastructure and communities (Beck et al. 2018).

Yet, over 80% of coral reefs in this region are threatened (Burke et al. 2012): *chronic* risks include overfishing, pollution, sediment runoff, and coastal developments; and *climate-* and *event-related* risks include bleaching events and tropical cyclones. Coral reef benefits in the region will only continue if these vital ecosystems are adequately protected and restored.

Protecting coral reefs includes work focused on effective management of coral reefs, restoration of degraded reefs, and repair of reefs damaged by disaster events, such as those after a natural hazard. Innovative sustainable finance instruments provide one avenue for funding such restoration and repair.

This report looks to the first-ever insurance policy taken out against coral reefs in 2019 in the state of Quintana Roo, Mexico, to highlight similar opportunities in Asia and the Pacific (The Nature Conservancy 2021a). In particular, this report reviews innovative financing instruments that may be available to fund reef restoration, reef management, and post-disaster reef repair, including insurance, bonds, and emergency funds. While these efforts require multiple funding sources working in tandem, this report focuses on opportunities for the application of a coral reef insurance policy in the region. This report will support engagement with key stakeholders—such as government ministries, local communities, and industries—and will help to build capacity to manage and reduce risks to reefs (and other coastal ecosystems) as a cost-effective strategy to enhance coastal resilience in Asian developing member countries.

For coral reefs, insurance payouts following a disaster event can be used to quickly fund the repair of damaged reefs to speed up recovery. In some instances, coral reefs may not be able to recover naturally without active restoration. But insurance is likely to be cost-effective—that is, the price of the premium payments is offset by the protective value provided by the coral reefs—in Fiji, Indonesia, the Philippines, and Solomon Islands, and other areas of Asia and the Pacific. While not exhaustive, these countries represent a starting point where a coral reef insurance pilot project could most likely be successfully developed and launched.

Ultimately, a comprehensive reef management system will include the financing of reef management, reef restoration, and post-disaster reef repair. Traditional sources of financing, such as government funds, grants, and tourism revenue, are typically insufficient to cover the full costs of a comprehensive reef management system (Hein and Staub 2021). Until sufficient funding is established, however, effective progress will not be made in reef management and restoration because a single disaster event can erase years or decades of progress. Coral reef insurance offers one innovative means of managing the risk to coral reefs from disaster events. Given the rapid loss and degradation of reefs, there is an urgent need to focus on identifying opportunities for and piloting reef insurance policies as a specific policy frequently takes months or years to develop.

INTRODUCTION

Coral reefs span an estimated 250,000 square kilometers across the world (Figure 1) (Burke et al. 2011a, 11).[1] The reefs protect coasts, provide food and income through commercial fisheries and tourism, and provide recreation opportunities. Nonetheless, more than 50% of coral reefs have been lost in the last 30 years and over 75% of the remaining are threatened by natural hazards or human activities (National Academies of Sciences, Engineering, and Medicine 2019; Burke et al. 2011a).

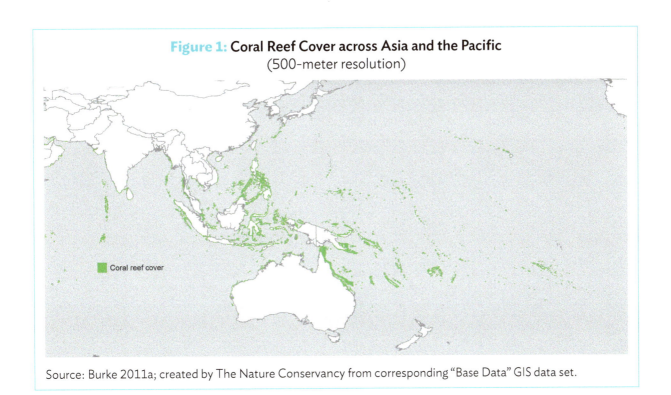

Figure 1: Coral Reef Cover across Asia and the Pacific
(500-meter resolution)

Source: Burke 2011a; created by The Nature Conservancy from corresponding "Base Data" GIS data set.

---

[1] In many regions, the exact spatially continuous distribution of live coral cover remains unknown (Asner et al. 2020).

Some of the largest of these reef systems are in Asia and the Pacific, and the majority of them are at risk. Current insufficient funding for their proper management and restoration calls for innovative financial schemes to do so.

This report focuses on such innovative financial schemes. Financial schemes can be established in advance of an event (*ex-ante*) or when an event occurs and financial need arises (*ex-post*). Ex-ante financial schemes are thought to be more efficient and effective than ex-post, in part because ex-ante financing can minimize disruption during great disturbances (Young and Wharton 2020). This report focuses on the potential in the region for coral reef insurance policies, a form of ex-ante financing.

The following sections review key information related to the feasibility of a coral reef insurance policy. The report first describes the benefits of coral reefs to onshore communities and the risks they face in disaster events due to natural hazards or human activities. It then discusses how to conduct post-damage reef restoration to expedite and improve recovery from damage. Subsequent sections describe insurance, in addition to other financial schemes, as an innovative financial scheme to fund restoration, and reveal the institutional capacity needed to implement it. Finally, the report looks at specific locations in Asia and the Pacific where such a policy may be feasible, focusing on Indonesia, the Philippines, Solomon Islands, and Fiji. It highlights opportunities for similar insurance schemes to cover other coastal ecosystems, such as mangroves, salt marshes, oysters, and sand dunes. The initial evidence is strong that such an insurance scheme in Asia and the Pacific may be feasible, although more work is needed.

II

BENEFITS OF CORAL REEFS

Across the world, over 850 million—or 12.5% of the world's population—live within 100 kilometers of a coral reef and over 275 million people live within 30 kilometers (Burke et al. 2011a, 11). In Asia and the Pacific, nearly 150 million people live within 30 kilometers of a coral reef and in the Pacific Island countries as much as 50% of the population lives within 30 kilometers (Burke et al. 2011a, 53–62). Coral reefs provide exceptionally valuable ecosystem services to these communities. They provide people with food, livelihoods, and economic opportunity and they protect shorelines from erosion and dissipate wave energy in storms.

Food and livelihoods: Many communities living close to reefs depend on them for food and livelihoods. Healthy coral reefs can sustain yields of between 5 and 15 tons of fish per square kilometer annually (Jennings and Polunin 1995, Maypa et al. 2002, Newton et al. 2007). In many countries in Asia and the Pacific, over 20% of daily protein needs come from marine fish, compared to a global average of under 5%.[2] Globally, over half of all coral reef fishers are estimated to reside in Asia and the Pacific—3.8 million out of 6.1 million (Teh, Teh, and Sumaila 2013). In some countries, such as across the Federated States of Micronesia, the Marshall Islands, and Tuvalu, over 25% of the entire population are reef fishers.[3] In Indonesia and the Philippines, nearly a million people are estimated to be coral reef fishers.[4] Gender distinctions can also be important within many fishing communities in Asia and the Pacific (Box 1).

Healthy coral reefs can sustain yields of between 5 and 15 tons of fish per square kilometer annually.

---

[2] Such countries include Kiribati, Malaysia, and Samoa. Estimates based on assumed minimum protein needs of 54 grams for a 150-pound adult. Food and Agriculture Organization. 2022. Food Balance Sheets. FAOSTAT (accessed 4 August 2022).

[3] See Teh et al. 2013 (supplementary table S3) and World Bank. World Development Indicators. DataBank (accessed 5 August 2022).

[4] See Teh et al. 2013 (supplementary table S3); and World Bank. World Development Indicators.

> **Box 1**

Gender Differences in Coral Reef Dependence

Women and men tend to rely on and use coral reefs in different ways because of local social structures and relations. For example, in many regions, women tend to fish for invertebrates on inshore reefs and intertidal zones while men fish in deeper waters.[a] This predominately female nearshore fishing activity, sometimes called "gleaning," is typically not accounted for in global fishing figures.[b]

Recently, scientists have used a stepwise approach to estimate small-scale fisheries production activities undertaken by women around the globe. They found that 2.1 million women, representing 11% of all small scale fishers globally, catch nearly 3 million tons of fish and invertebrates annually.[b] Female participation rates were highest in Oceania, where more than 25% of all small-scale fishers are women.[b] Indeed, women are found to be involved in nearly every step of the fisheries value chain.[c]

In Asia and the Pacific, coral reefs are critical for fishing. Thus, understanding the role of women in small-scale fisheries will be vital for any effort to protect and restore coral reefs, as these efforts will inevitably impact local fishing communities. Fisheries management will need to consider both the high-value market-oriented species typically fished by men alongside the supporting ecosystems where women typically fish.[c] Going forward, gender-transformative approaches—that is, approaches that target the structural causes and symptoms of gender inequality—will be needed to effectively implement fisheries management practices to protect and restore coral reefs.[d]

[a] Lau and Ruano-Chamorro 2021; Torell et al. 2021.
[b] Harper et al. 2020.
[c] Torell et al. 2021.
[d] Lau and Ruano-Chamorro 2021.

Tourism: Divers, snorkelers, fishers, and tourists from around the world seek out the recreation coral reefs offer, sustaining tourism in many tropical countries. Globally, over 100 countries benefit from coral-reef-associated tourism, with a total estimated global value of $36 billion (Spalding et al. 2017, 104). Many areas of Asia and the Pacific have a coral-reef-associated tourism value that exceeds $900,000 per square kilometer (Figure 2). In addition to direct coral reef-associated tourism, carbonate production on coral reefs aids in the provision and replenishment of beach sand, another main driver of coastal tourism (Andersson and Gledhill 2013).

> Globally, over 100 countries benefit from coral-reef-associated tourism, with a total estimated global value of $36 billion.

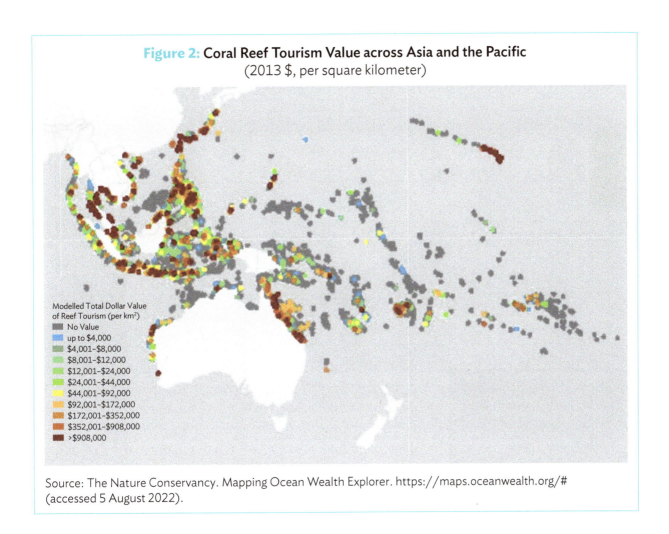

Source: The Nature Conservancy. Mapping Ocean Wealth Explorer. https://maps.oceanwealth.org/# (accessed 5 August 2022).

Coastal protection: Beyond their biological and aesthetic value, the physical structures of coral reefs serve as natural, submerged breakwaters. Coral reefs can dissipate as much as 97% of wave energy, which can reduce erosion and flooding and prevent wave damage during tropical storms (Figure 3) (Ferrario et al. 2014). Across all 71,000 square kilometers of coral reef coastlines globally, the reefs reduce the annual expected damage from storm events by as much as $4 billion (Beck et al. 2018, 3). In Asia and the Pacific, coral reefs provide hundreds of millions in annual expected flood protection benefits in Malaysia ($452 million), the Philippines ($590 million), and Indonesia ($639 million) (Beck et al. 2018, Table 1).

> Across all 71,000 square kilometers of coral reef coastlines globally, the reefs reduce the annual expected damage from storm events by as much as $4 billion.

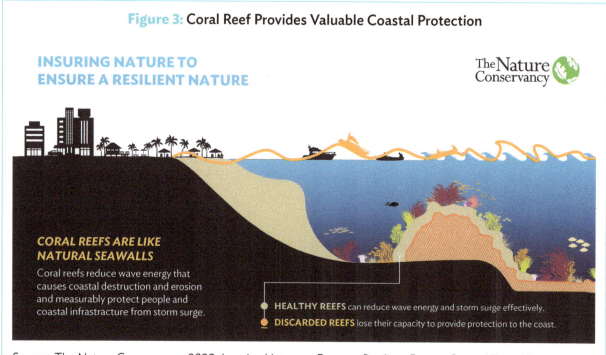

Figure 3: Coral Reef Provides Valuable Coastal Protection

Source: The Nature Conservancy. 2022. Insuring Nature to Ensure a Resilient Future: Coastal Zone Management Trust. https://www.nature.org/content/dam/tnc/nature/en/documents/TNC-CoastalManagementTrust_Infographic_04.pdf (accessed 8 August 2022).

Coral reefs also host a quarter of all known marine species and play a critical role in the broader health of coastal ecosystems (Hoegh-Guldberg 1999, Moberg and Folk 1999, Spalding et al. 2017). Asia and the Pacific has the highest concentration of coral and reef fish species on the globe (Burke et al. 2012). At the same time, more than 60% of the world's reefs are under immediate and direct risk from one or more local sources (e.g., overfishing, coastal development, and pollution), and many reefs are thus degraded and unable to provide the vital services on which so many people depend (Burke et al. 2011a).

More than 60% of the world's reefs are under immediate and direct risk from one or more local sources.

RISKS FACED BY CORAL REEFS AND THEIR IMPACTS

Global risks, such as climate change, and local risks, such as overfishing, have collectively contributed to the loss of more than 50% of coral reefs over the last 30 years (National Academies of Sciences 2019). A review of 16 different risks to reefs globally assessed their impact based on type of risk, duration of event, and impact on coral reefs (Figure 4). The review documented annual change in live coral cover following the onset of the risk from 157 different studies spanning 1,097 coral reef sites globally (Alvarez-Filip et al. 2021). The study showed that, for example, earthquakes can affect up to 1,000 kilometers of coral reefs and can destroy nearly all live coral cover (Figure 4). In contrast, dredging will impact less area, only up to 1 kilometer, and destroy a smaller percentage of the live coral cover (Figure 4).

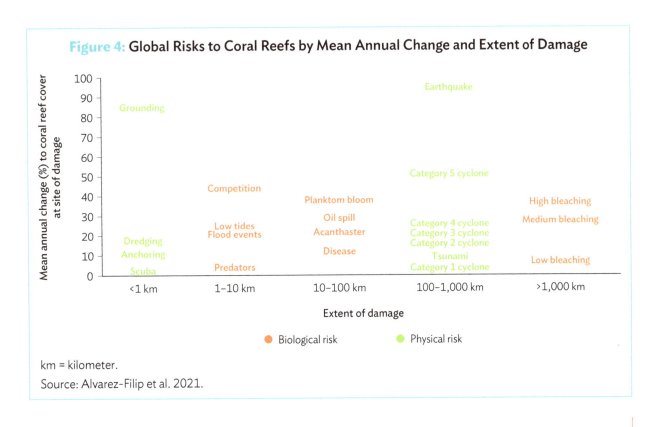

Figure 4: Global Risks to Coral Reefs by Mean Annual Change and Extent of Damage

km = kilometer.
Source: Alvarez-Filip et al. 2021.

Table 1 details a subset of these acute stressors (or pulse stressors).

Table 1: Description of Subset of Acute Stressors Faced by Coral Reefs Globally

Risk	Description
Ship groundings	Accidental ship groundings or strandings on coral reefs can damage the reefs in very specific areas.[a] This can seriously damage the reef's structure and destroy habitat for organisms. The flattening of topography during groundings creates sand and rubble that is carried over the area and disturbs the settlement, growth, and survival of bottom-dwelling creatures. Corals are able to repopulate damaged areas; indeed, they can populate the ship structures. Yet, slow growth and high mortality may feed a cycle of settlement and mortality that means there is little or extremely slow growth progress.[b]
Tropical storms/cyclones	Powerful tropical storms can change coral reefs. As natural phenomena with differing characteristics, damage to reefs can vary—from mild to complete reef loss.[c] Abrasion, fracture, and colony detachment during the storms can kill large amounts of coral and the debris and pollution further damage the reefs during high winds and flooding.[d]
Coral bleaching	During unusually warm conditions—because corals are highly sensitive to temperature, and "bleach" when stressed by warming seas—they lose the microscopic algae that usually live within their tissues.[e] This can kill the corals, depending on the duration and degree of the event. Increases in ocean temperatures, rising sea levels, and other climate impacts are predicted to heighten the intensity and severity of coral bleaching events. Ocean warming can also exacerbate stressors such as coral disease.[f] In addition, while coral bleaching is an acute stressor, background increases in ocean temperatures are causing chronic stress to many reef systems.
Oil spills	Corals are also being killed when petroleum leaks into the sea and the heavy oil mixes with sand or sediment, eventually sinking and smothering corals. Prolonged exposure can also hinder coral reproduction, growth, behavior, and development.[g]
Disease	When disease strikes the coral, its assault on the living tissues can kill part or all of a colony. Although diseases are natural and commonly found in coral reefs, disease outbreak frequency is increasing, such as the Stony Coral Tissue Loss Disease in Florida and the Caribbean.[h] Land-based pollution and global climate issues are also raised diseases incidence among corals.[i]
Anchor impacts	Boats and ships, when they drop anchor, can break coral colonies. The damage is generally in a limited area, but dragging the anchor, as occurs sometimes, may damage the corals for hundreds of meters.[j]
Tsunamis	When an earthquake below the ocean occurs, it may cause a tsunami, and the force of the waves generated can be strong enough to break coral colonies. Likewise, tons of heavy debris may be dragged through the corals by the as they recede. Similarly, sludge can bury and suffocate the coral.[k]

[a] Byrnes and Dunn 2020.
[b] Moulding, Kosmynin, and Gilliam 2012.
[c] Pérez-Cervantes et al. 2020.
[d] Burke et al. 2011a.
[e] Burke et al. 2011a (4).
[f] Veron et al. 2009.
[g] Turner and Renegar 2017.
[h] Harvell et al. 2007 and Precht et al. 2016.
[i] Vega Thurber et al. 2014.
[j] Byrnes and Dunn 2020, and Forrester et al. 2015.
[k] Majumdar et al. 2018.

Note: Risks are ordered by mean annual change in live coral cover. See Alvarez-Filip et al. 2021 (Figure 28).
Source: Information in table compiled by The Nature Conservancy.

Other risks to reefs are chronic (or press disturbances) and continually impact coral reefs (as listed in Table 2). It is important to note that some of the acute stressors, such as coral bleaching, could become chronic stressors as a result of climate change.

Table 2: Description of Chronic Stressor Faced by Coral Reefs Globally

Risk	Description
Coastal construction	Human settlements, industry, aquaculture, or infrastructure in coastal zones has large impacts on its ecosystems. Dredging or land filling can cause direct physical damage, while factors such as increased runoff of sediment, pollution, and sewage damage the reefs indirectly. Coastal development may also see coastal vegetation removed, such as mangroves and coastal dunes. These ecosystems trap sediment and thus prevent damage to coastal ecosystems, so when removed, that protection is lost. Coastal developments threaten almost 25% of the world's reefs, of which more than 10% face a high threat.[a]
Overfishing	Growing human populations and increasing demands from tourism and international markets have significantly impacted fish stocks. Overfishing has been identified as the most pervasive of all local threats to coral reefs; it can reduce both target and non-target fish populations, even to the point of extinction.[a] Removing just one group of fish can have cascading effects across the ecosystem.[b] Coral reef ecosystems rely on fish species, such as herbivores, for healthy functioning.
Destructive fishing	Destructive fishing methods include dynamite, gill nets, and beach seines. These methods harm coral reefs not just through physical impacts but also through by-catch and mortality of non-target species including juveniles. Although illegal in many countries, dynamite fishing remains a persistent threat, particularly in Southeast Asia and East Africa.[c] Destructive fishing could be an acute stressor if it occurs in singular instances and becomes a chronic stressor as it continually occurs in a similar location.
Unsustainable tourism	As hotels emerge in remote locations, bringing construction, sewage, and waste, it can threaten reefs. Tour boats can pollute coastal waters through the discharge of fuel, human waste, and grey water or spread invasive species through transportation of ballast water and hull fouling of cruise ships. Tourists can also directly engage in high-impact recreational activities, such as feeding marine life, disposing of trash in the marine environment, and generating sediments on the reef and breakage of coral by direct contact such as walking, touching, kicking, standing, or inappropriate diving and snorkeling practices.[d]
Pollution	Pollution frequently emerges alongside development of coastal areas. Sewage is the most widespread pollutant, and elevated nutrient levels present in sewage encourage blooms of plankton that block light and encourage growth of seaweeds that compete for space on the reef.[e] Many countries with coral reefs have little to no sewage treatment; the Caribbean, Southeast Asia, and Pacific regions discharge an estimated 80% to 90% of their wastewater untreated.[f] Toxic chemicals are also a problem. Sources of toxic chemicals in coastal runoff include industries, aquaculture, and agriculture, as well as households, parking lots, and gardens.[a]

[a] Burke et al. 2011a.
[b] Mumby et al. 2006.
[c] Fox et al. 2000.
[d] Jackson et al. 2014.
[e] Reopanichkul et al. 2009.
[f] UNEP/GPA 2006.
Source: Information in table compiled by The Nature Conservancy.

A. Risks Coral Reefs Face in Asia and the Pacific

Threats to coral reefs in the region are much higher than the global average; more than 85% of coral reefs in Asia and the Pacific are threatened by local sources compared to the global average of 60% (Burke et al. 2012).

Overfishing, including destructive fishing, is the most pervasive and damaging threat to coral reefs in Asia and the Pacific (Burke et al. 2012). Destructive fishing is common throughout much of Asia and the Pacific, particularly in the Philippines and Indonesia, threatening nearly 60% of the region's reefs (Burke et al. 2012). Threats from land-based sources, such as watershed-based pollution or coastal development, represent an additional threat to over one-third of the region's coral reefs (Burke et al. 2012). Many coral reefs in the region are impacted by not just one but a combination of these local threats.

In addition, projected increases in ocean temperature and acidity, bleaching events, increased intensity of cyclones and typhoons, and changes in rainfall patterns (prolonged flood and drought cycles) are predicted to have major impacts on coastal ecosystems in the region (Hoegh-Guldberg et al. 2009). Indeed, substantial evidence suggests these impacts already being seen; coral bleaching events have become more common and rising sea levels are threatening mangroves (Hoegh-Guldberg et al. 2009). The only clear solution to rising ocean temperatures and other climate-change-related impacts will be a concerted global effort to reduce atmospheric greenhouse gas emissions. However, reducing or eliminating local threats (e.g., pollution and overfishing) can help support reef resilience (Burke et al. 2011a, 4).

While cyclones are more prevalent in the tropical Atlantic and central Indo-Pacific, compared with the eastern and western Indo-Pacific, the reefs of Asia and the Pacific are particularly sensitive because of the extent to which they are already threatened by local stressors (Alvarez-Filip 2021). Global climate models do not consistently predict change in the location or frequency of tropical cyclones/typhoons as temperatures rise. However, the models do all point to more intense storms (higher maximum wind speeds and heavier rainfall) (Hoegh-Guldberg et al. 2009). Large parts of Asia and the Pacific lie outside the cyclone/typhoon belts and may be unaffected. However, Bangladesh, the Federated States of Micronesia, Fiji, Guam, India, Palau, the People's Republic of China, the Philippines, Solomon Islands, and Viet Nam are some of the countries more commonly impacted by typhoons and cyclones and are likely to experience changes in their intensity and impact in the decades ahead (Figure 5).[5] Typhoon Yolanda, which was one of the most powerful tropical cyclones ever recorded, had sustained wind speeds close to 250 kilometers per hour, 12-meter waves, and caused billions of dollars in damage to the Philippines (Box 2).

---

[5] Hoegh-Guldberg et al. 2009 and Reliefweb 2019.

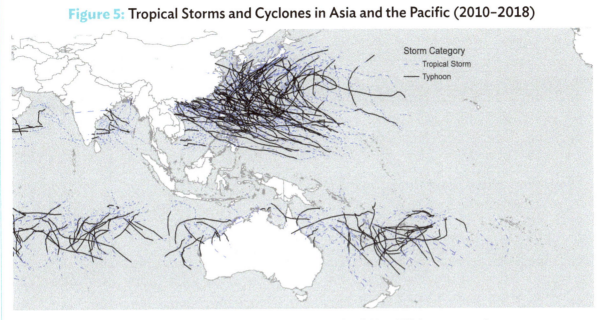

Figure 5: Tropical Storms and Cyclones in Asia and the Pacific (2010–2018)

Notes: Tropical storm refers to storms with maximum wind speeds of 63–117 kilometers per hour.
A typhoon refers to storms with maximum wind speeds of 118 kilometers per hour or more.
Source: Reliefweb 2019.

Box 2

Typhoon Yolanda in the Philippines

Typhoon Yolanda, internationally known as Haiyan, was the strongest typhoon ever to make landfall in the Philippines. Yolanda entered the Philippine Area of Responsibility on 8 November 2013, and made landfall six different times in the country.[a] It destroyed about 600,000 houses, killed 6,300 people, and displaced over 4 million people.[b] Observers estimated losses in infrastructure, social structures, and production from $1 billion–$10.5 billion.

To quantify the impacts of Yolanda on coral reefs, Anticamara and Go (2017) compared coral cover and diversity, fish abundance, biomass, and diversity between sites before and after Yolanda. They found that some reef areas were completely wiped out (high dead coral covzer ranging from 20% to 60%) with decreases in coral species richness. Even though the impact on the reefs was high, most reefs in the area had already suffered degradation prior to Yolanda (i.e., due to overfishing, destructive fishing, and siltation from land). The study also showed reductions in fish abundance and low fish biomass across all the study sites after Yolanda.

Unfortunately, the damaged coral cover and the low fisheries production status indicate that an increase in fishing pressure combined with the anticipated increase in the frequency and intensity of typhoons could cause a more extreme collapse in the coastal ecosystems of the area than even the one caused by Yolanda.

[a] USAID. Typhoon Haiyan/Yolanda Infographic (accessed 9 August 2022).
[b] Anticamara and Go 2017.

Much of Asia and the Pacific also overlaps with the Ring of Fire, a region of the Pacific Ocean where many volcanic eruptions and earthquakes occur. Volcanic eruptions deliver hot magma that forms igneous rock of varying composition, as well as volcanic ash, to the nearshore waters (Houk 2011, Le Bas and Streckeisen 1991). Both the rock and ash can smother vast expanses of living coral reefs rapidly (Pandolfi et al. 2006). In addition, volcanic ash particles contain numerous minerals in high concentrations that influence surrounding waters over the long term; most notably, iron, magnesium, and silica (Flaathen and Gislason 2007).

B. Economic Returns of Healthy Coral Reefs in Asia and the Pacific

In 2018, the United Nations Environment Programme, International Sustainability Unit, International Coral Reef Initiative, and Trucost modeled a comparison of expected returns to each of the key sectors in Asia and the Pacific (tourism, commercial fisheries, and coastal development) from 2017 to 2030 under a future healthy reef scenario or a degraded reef scenario.[6] The results showed annualized total economic returns in the region under a healthy reefs scenario of $16.1 billion compared to $13.5 billion under a degraded scenario. Annualized economic returns across tourism, commercial fisheries, and coastal development were $0.4 million to $1.7 million higher under the healthy reef scenario compared to the degraded scenario, with tourism showing the largest benefits from healthy reefs (Table 3).

Table 3: Value of Economic Returns from Asia and the Pacific, Estimated 2030 and Annualized 2017–2030
($ million, 2017 prices)

Scenario		Tourism	Commercial Fisheries	Coastal Development	Total
Healthy reef scenario	Annualized (2017)	$7,040	$6,365	$2,675	$16,081
	Estimated (2030)	$8,520	$6,942	$3,124	$18,586
Degraded reef scenario	Annualized (2017)	$5,312	$5,971	$2,178	$13,461
	Estimated (2030)	$4,145	$6,940	$1,866	$12,105

Source: United Nations Environment Programme, International Sustainability Unit, International Coral Reef Initiative, and Trucost (2018).

The trend in changes in economic returns under the healthy and degraded scenarios is driven primarily by the rate of change in live coral cover, which, in turn, is directly related to the threats and risks to the reefs. These three sectors represent just part of the broader economic returns that may accrue to other sectors linked to coral reefs, and the social and environmental benefits that may be lost as coral reefs are degraded.

---

[6] Healthy reef scenario and degraded reef scenario are defined in terms of changes in live coral cover, which was identified more broadly as a key marker of coral reef health. United Nations Environment Programme, International Sustainability Unit, International Coral Reef Initiative, and Trucost (2018).

ADDRESSING CORAL REEF DAMAGE

After damage to coral reefs has occurred, active restoration and repair of the reefs is often needed to ensure they are able to fully recover. For example, following a tropical cyclone, immediate response (within 90 days of the storm) greatly increases the chance that the coral will recover and survive. In addition, medium- to long-term restoration efforts might be necessary. Reef restorations after major tropical cyclones can last as much as 2 to 5 years after the storm has passed.

To restore a reef, coral colonies are reproduced through sexual propagation and from fragments. Reef restoration may also include consolidation of broken reef and management of snorkelers, divers, water pollution, fishing, and other stressors. New discoveries, scientific and on the ground, have improved such efforts, and managers and community practitioners have employed more low-cost and low-tech approaches. Methods of reef restoration—asexual and sexual, propagation and physical reef restoration—are described as follows:

A. Asexual and Sexual Propagation

Reef restoration projects to date have mostly transplanted corals propagated in intermediate nurseries to bring cover back to degraded reefs (Guest et al. 2014). Transplants can be produced asexually (culturing fragments from donor colonies) or sexually (collecting and rearing larvae or gametes from reproductively mature colonies). Asexual propagation has been implemented for decades with well-established techniques for many species and locations, whereas sexual propagation is at the pilot stage (Boström-Einarsson et al. 2020; Guest et al. 2010; Randall et al. 2020; and Shafir, Van Rijn, and Rinkevich 2006). Each method has its advantages and disadvantages (Table 4) and each manager must evaluate how a combination of different approaches meets needs, capacities, and funding.

Table 4: Benefits and Limitations of Asexual and Sexual Propagation Methods

	Asexual Propagation	Sexual Propagation
Benefits	• With little training needed, asexual propagation is likely cheaper and less labor intensive than sexual propagation.[a] • Can be an important community outreach activity because it can be implemented with simple methods and can engage locals and tourists in reef conservation.[b]	• Less need to fragment donor colonies, thus reducing collateral damage to source reefs.[c] • Transplants obtained through sexual propagation have greater genotypic diversity and greater resilience.[d] • Can affect restoration at the reef scale in a single treatment.
Limitations	• Does not promote genetic diversity because fragments are genetically identical to the parent coral.[a]	• Can require hatchery facilities and expertise in larval-rearing techniques.[e] • Limited to natural spawning times/events in the field.

[a] Zepeda et al. 2018.
[b] Jantzen 2016.
[c] Edwards and Gomez 2007.
[d] Devlin-Durante et al. 2016, Guest et al. 2014, and Edwards and Gomez 2007.
[e] Epstein, Bak, and Rinkevich 2001; Omori 2011; Guest et al. 2014; and Edwards and Gomez 2007.
Source: Information in table compiled by The Nature Conservancy.

Asexual Propagation

Asexual coral colony propagation methods use fragments of corals from donor colonies or corals in the wild that have been broken, for example, by storms or vessel grounding (often termed "corals of opportunity") (Zepeda et al. 2018). Reattaching these broken fragments to existing corals or other substrates supports growth and maintenance of coral populations (Box 3) (Chavanich et al. 2014). Asexual propagation often involves using a small piece of coral (≤ 5 centimeters) from a donor colony (collected or clipped) and maintained in nurseries (land-based or ocean-based) and protected from reef stressors (National Marine Fisheries Service 2016). The goals of asexual propagation include: (i) to maximize benefits from a given amount of source material and thus minimize damage to donor areas; (ii) to establish small colonies from fragments, which should survive better than the fragments would have done if simply transplanted directly onto a reef; and (iii) to have banks of small corals readily available for transplant in the event of an impact such as a ship grounding (Edwards and Gomez 2007). Success of asexual propagation methods in restoration projects varies by methods implemented and the conditions at the local sites (Zepeda et al. 2018). Factors that may cause coral mortality following transplantation include storm damage, bleaching events, disease, predation, and poor water quality; thus effectively managing local stressors and monitoring current and future impacts is essential (Young, Schopmeyer, and Lirman 2012; Zepeda et al. 2018).

Sexual Propagation

Sexual and asexual propagation differ in two major ways (Jantzen 2016). First, sexual propagation requires nurturing the vulnerable corals, after fertilization, through the early life stages.
Second, each of these corals propagated this way is genetically unique (Zepeda et al. 2018).

Sexual reproduction also creates coral recruits that can be grown in nurseries (land-based or ocean-based). They can then be "planted" in restoration areas. Coral settlement and transplantation have benefited from recent advances in sexual propagation (dela Cruz and Harrison 2017, Okamoto et al. 2008, Guest et al. 2010, Nakamura et al. 2011). Using collecting nets, the gametes (eggs and sperm) are captured during natural coral spawning events (Box 3). The collected gametes are fertilized, with many different combinations of genes (Zepeda et al. 2018).

Box 3

Reef Restoration in the Philippines

The Mead Foundation, Inc. is a registered nongovernment organization in the Philippines focused on integrated marine conservation. Pressure on natural resources in the Philippines tends to be highly correlated to financial insecurity and, as such, the foundation's holistic approach includes restoration and conservation, sustainable and scalable programs, education, and awareness programs for all stakeholders, as well as sustainable livelihood creation.

Coral restoration is a core program for the integrated approach, though there is no one-size-fits-all and the most suitable technique will be applied to the specific project area. The foundation undertakes both coral fragmentation and coral spawning restoration techniques. Both techniques have different strategies, required resources, implementation time frames, and scale potential.

Coral fragmentation is a technique where corals that have been broken by natural or human activity are collected and placed in undersea coral nurseries. These rescued corals, known as corals of opportunity, are still alive when collected from the sea floor but will die if not taken to the nursery. Competent corals are never taken from the reef. The nurseries are tethered to the sand, with floats at the top which provides for a flexible structure that moves with the current and suspends the corals in the water column. Once mature, often in as little as 6 months, the corals are taken from the nursery and re-fragmented; these fragments can be returned to additional coral nurseries for further propagation or placed back onto natural or artificial reef substrate using non-toxic marine epoxy. From this point, the reef will continue to reproduce naturally. This technique is shown to be very successful for acute, rapid reef restoration. It does, however, require significant scuba diving resources so it can be more expensive than other techniques.

Coral larval restoration is a relatively new approach developed by Professor Peter Harrison of Southern Cross University. This technique harnesses the synchronized annual coral spawning events whereby coral colonies release their eggs and sperm in unison. In nature, once released, the spawn floats to the surface, forming slicks where the coral eggs are fertilized before naturally setting back onto the reef. Under this coral larval technique, coral colonies are identified that have shown resilience to coral bleaching. Then, prior to annual coral spawning events, nests are placed over selected corals permitting the spawn to be captured, held in floating and onshore nurseries, before being settled back over degraded reef areas. This approach facilitates the targeted placement of genetically stronger corals over areas needing rehabilitation. This technique is being successfully employed on the Great Barrier Reef and in the Philippines and promises the ability to restore larger areas of reef at lower cost.

Sources: Ben Mead, The Mead Foundation; Harrison et al. 2021; Boström-Einarsson et al. 2020; and Randall et al. 2020.

B. Physical Reef Restoration

A damaged or degraded coral reef, or one where coral larval settlement is unsuitable, may call for restoration of the physical structure or substrate of the reef (Zepeda et al. 2018). Ship groundings and coral mining can cause severe physical impact to the reef crest, as can blast fishing and major storm events. Such trauma can kill coral and coralline algae and destabilize the coral rubble and sand and reduce overall reef rugosity (Edwards and Gomez 2007, World Bank 2016).[7]

In restoration of a reef, this can involve restoration or creation of new reef structures. This is often done using limestone and cement in combination. The addition of structural integrity to the reef under this method enhances it (Zepeda et al. 2018). Reef recovery, meanwhile, can be hastened by adding to the substrate to replicate reef structures (Zepeda et al. 2018). In addition, when damaged, an unstable bottom is not suitable for settlement and growth of corals and likely explains why damaged sites do not recover naturally (Miller, McFall, and Hulbert 1993). Physical reef restoration includes:

Repairing the reef: Applying cement or epoxy to large cracks in the reef framework, or righting and re-attaching stony and/or branching corals, soft corals, sponges, and other reef organisms (Zepeda et al. 2018).

Replacing damaged or lost reef structures: Where reef relief and rugosity has been lost by degradation or by direct physical impact, dead coral rubble and/or rock piles can be placed on the seafloor to create substrate for corals to settle and grow and/or to replace the lost three-dimensional structure of the reef (Edwards and Gomez 2007, Zepeda et al. 2018).

Stabilizing damaged reef structures: Manmade materials (e.g., cement, wire, string, biodegradable nets) can be used to stabilize the reef framework and reduce the negative effects of unconsolidated rubble on coral settlement and growth (Zepeda et al. 2018).

Box 4 looks at some of these restoration approaches applied in Komodo National Park in Indonesia.

For some impacts, a combination physical and biological interventions may be required for effective reef restoration (Edwards and Gomez 2007, Boström-Einarsson et al. 2020, Shaver et al. 2022). Prior to determining which interventions are most appropriate for a specific area, an assessment of the environmental conditions needs to be carried out. For example, sites that present cases of bleaching may need heat-resistant fragments to be transplanted. Sites that present cases of sediment runoff will need to have the sediment pollution addressed before planting corals.

---

[7] Reef rugosity is a commonly used measure of the surface roughness of coral reefs. When a coral reef has a higher level of reef rugosity, corals are more easily able to attach and grow on more elevated substrata.

Substrate Stabilization from Reef Recovery from Blast Fishing in Komodo National Park, 1998–2008

Blast fishing in Komodo National Park, Indonesia, ongoing since the 1950s, damaged something like half of coral reefs in the 1,817-square-kilometer area. In response in 1995, park authorities began patrolling the area, cutting the destructive fishing technique by 80%. Heavily blasted sites, nonetheless, did not naturally recover with the initial patrolling program, even though coral larvae were numerous in good quality water. Dead coral fragments and other rubble scraped and smothered new coral recruits, killing many of the juvenile coral and holding back coral growth.

Park officials responded by stabilizing the substrate to increase hard coral coverage and marine biodiversity in the blasted areas. They did so using low-cost, low-tech techniques.

The pilot study tried out three methods for stabilizing the rubble: netting (5-centimeter mesh fishing net), concrete slabs, and rock piles, with corals initially recruited under all three. However, rubble eventually covered the netting and the concrete slabs were often overturned. The rock piles too were filled by rubble, but they could be made larger and were built up above the rubble fields, and with this promise, were used for larger scale restoration. Fish congregated quickly around rock piles after installation.

In 6 years, live coral cover had increased substantially, even around the least successful sites. On untreated blast sites, there was no natural regeneration of coral. Hard coral coverage of the rocks was as high as 43% at the most successful sites.

Source: Fox et al. 2005.

C. Artificial Reef Creation

Artificial reefs (those made by humans), low-crested structures in particular, have gained a reputation for their innovative protection of coastal areas worldwide (Zepeda et al. 2018). In areas where underwater structures are used, (i) topographic complexity increases right away and (ii) substrate are stabilized for coral and other invertebrate settlement (or for coral transplantation). These efforts also provide (iii) hard structures that can hamper damaging net based fishing techniques (including trawling and seine net fishing) and (iv) new sites for scuba divers, taking high diving pressure on natural reefs. The underwater structures also provide (v) additional area for fish populations and (vi) sea defense services (Edwards and Gomez 2007).

Among physical structures, meanwhile, structural stability is better using prefabricated concrete than submerged rocks. Nonetheless, the former can be costly and intrusive on the reef ecosystem (Muttray and Reedijk 2009). Some concrete structures require specific placement, whereas others can be randomly placed, and stability will vary depending on their typology (i.e., the structure's weight or friction between different units of concrete) (Zepeda et al. 2018). Table 5 presents examples.

Table 5: Commonly Used Physical Structures

Name	Characteristics
Reef balls	Hollow structures of semicircular or semispherical prefabricated concrete pieces with holes in their walls. The module cavities form feeding currents, in which fish proliferate. Design often also includes attachment points for coral transplants. Reef balls are one of the most commonly implemented methods and are increasingly applied for submerged breakwaters.
EcoReefs	The snowflakes shape of these ceramic structures maximize vertical surface. This encourages coral recruitment and fish habitat. The shape also aims for a "hydrodynamic current field" that encourages coral settlement and feeding. Commonly used in nursery culture.
Wave attenuation devices	Pyramid-shaped breakwater that can be triangular or parallelepiped with greater hydraulic efficiency in relation to other types of breakwaters. They require less concrete to build and can favor the settlement of marine organisms.

Reef balls. Photo taken from Blundell 2010; **EcoReefs.** Photo taken from Chiu-Freund 2009; and **WADS.** Photo from Douglas et al. 2012.
Sources: Fabian, Beck, and Potts 2013; Muttray and Reedijk 2009; and Zepeda et al. 2018.

If it is suitable to use concrete structures, several characteristics should guide choice, based on the most efficient and cost-efficient unit. The module's hydraulic and structural stability, for example. Also important are the method of manufacture; the manipulation required for use, as installation and maintenance requirement; and unit longevity. Most concrete structures can last 20 to 50 years and provide sea defense services that may vary from $1 million to $10 million per kilometer depending on the shoreline (Edwards and Gomez 2007, Zepeda et al. 2018). Physical structures can provide significant coastal protection benefits, but if planned and designed inadequately, engineered structures can also cause environmental damage by removing natural habitat and altering circulation and sediment transport to adjacent habitats (Chapman and Underwood 2011). Recent technological advances have accelerated the pace at which physical structures can promote reef growth and development (Box 5).

Mars Assisted Reef Restoration System

Mars Sustainable Solutions (MSS) has been working in Indonesia since 2006 to develop effective coral reef restoration techniques. Many of the reefs in the Spermonde Archipelago, a group of over 100 islands off the southwest coast of Sulawesi, have been severely degraded by destructive fishing and coral mining. MSS developed the Mars Assisted Reef Restoration System to restore the degraded reefs in the archipelago, in partnership with local and international collaborators.

The system creates "reef stars" using locally fabricated steel structures to which locally sourced coral fragments can be attached. These reef stars are then anchored to the reef bed in a web-like structure around existing coral outcrops. This web is then further anchored to the reef using steel stakes, making it highly resistant to wave energy. Over time, corals are able to grow out of the web in three directions—up, out, and down—and the reef stars can virtually disappear in as little as 4 years. While the system was initially piloted in Indonesia, it has more recently been deployed on the Great Barrier Reef, in Maldives, and on the Mexican Mesoamerican Reef.

Sources: Smith 2022; Williams et al. 2019.

D. Emergency Restoration

While some risks to reefs, such as poor water quality and overfishing, require long-term management actions to mitigate, acute events (e.g., strong storms, ship grounding) often require immediate emergency responses to rescue coral colonies and repair a reef. Emergency restoration involves biological and physical restoration actions, typically within a short time frame. Emergency restoration also frequently involves debris cleanup in addition to coral planting.

Rapid and effective restoration following acute event helps ensure that coral colonies and reefs remain intact and are able to continue to benefit coastal communities. Zepeda et al. (2019) developed the Early Warning and Rapid Response Protocol, which presents six steps to guide first responders and reef managers on actions to be taken before, during, and after a tropical cyclone to mitigate the impacts on coral reefs.[8] Some of the restoration actions included as part of the primary and secondary responses (step 4 and step 5, respectively) are listed as follows;

- Remove all debris from the reef generated by a cyclone.
- Reattach displaced, dislodged, broken, or overturned massive boulder colonies or fragments.
- Remove colonies buried under the sand.

---

[8] A first responder is a diver or snorkeler with specialized training to assess and provide aid to the reef after a tropical cyclone. They work in teams called brigades that are responsible for implementing the rapid response and emergency post-storm reef restoration (Zepeda et al. 2019).

- Remove and stabilize loose, dead coral and sediment, which are damaging the reef.
- Place rescued coral fragments into nurseries.
- Assist reef managers with the maintenance and monitoring of nurseries and sites rehabilitated after the cyclone.

Ultimately, one must understand which restoration and management actions are best suited to address the risks and damage to any particular reef (Figure 6). Stakeholders will make the best restoration and management decisions if they have a clear understanding of the value of the goods and services provided by the reefs (Chavanich et al. 2014). In addition, support from all stakeholders, local and global, is necessary for restoration and management efforts to succeed (Burke et al. 2011a). The promotion and adoption of environmental policies and regulations may also be needed to increase public awareness and attention to effective implementation. Finally, the financing of restoration and management actions likely requires multiple financial schemes and diversified sources of revenue (Spergel and Moye 2004).

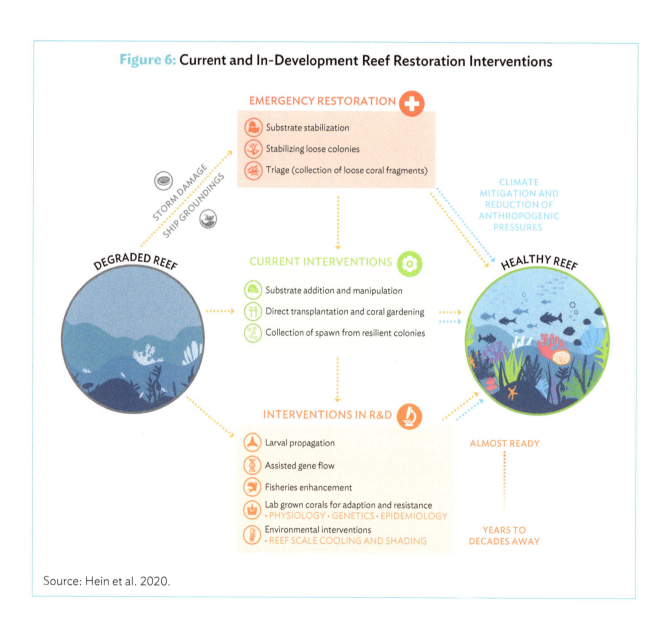

Figure 6: Current and In-Development Reef Restoration Interventions

Source: Hein et al. 2020.

V
INNOVATIVE FINANCING FOR MANAGING RISKS TO CORAL REEFS

A range of financial schemes and funding sources can be used to manage risks to coral reefs. Traditionally, sources such as government funds, grants, and tourism revenue have been used to fund coral reef restoration and repair (Table 6) (Hein and Staub 2021). These traditional sources, however, are frequently not enough to cover the full restoration and repair of coral reefs. In more recent years, increasing focus has been placed on developing innovative funding sources, such as insurance, to complement these traditional sources of funding. This section focuses on these innovative funding sources.

Table 6: Traditional Funding Sources Supporting Reef Restoration and Repair

Funding Source	Example Revenue Stream	Funding Source	Example Revenue Stream
Government	• Direct allocation • Bonds and taxes • Lotteries, stamps, and license plates • Concession • Real estate tax surcharges • Debt relief • National, state and local development banks' loans	Tourism revenue	• Protected area entry fees • Diving or yachting fees • Airport passenger or cruise ship fees • Hotel taxes • Voluntary donations • Merchandise sales/gift shop • Concessions
Grant revenue	• Bilateral and multilateral donors • Private foundations • Nongovernment organizations • Conservation trust funds	Fishing revenue	• License and permit sales • Quotas • Catch levies • Fines
		Energy and mining	• Oil spill funds • Right-of-way pipelines • Royalties
		Private sector contributions	• Corporate donations • Local business donations

Source: Reef Resilience Network 2022.

For this document, financial mechanisms generate, manage, structure, intermediate, and/or deploy financing to support a range of issues including, but not limited to, sustainable development and poverty alleviation, disaster risk reduction, climate change adaptation and mitigation, biodiversity loss, or the development and growth of blue economies. Financial mechanisms can be global, regional, national, or subnational in scope.[9] Financial mechanisms can play a critical role in advancing both the development and deployment of other innovative funding sources. Innovative financing sources include insurance, bonds, investment loans, and other lines of credit.

The following discusses how insurance can be used as an innovative financing instrument to effectively manage risk to coral reefs. It summarizes a suite of alternative innovative financing instruments, such as debt-for-nature swaps, that may be used independently or in concert with insurance or other funding sources. Careful consideration must be given to the context in which the funding source will be deployed and the applicability of the source to the context, since each funding source presents unique opportunities and limitations. Ultimately, the goal should be to select the funding source, or a set of synergistic sources, to achieve intended outcomes and manage coral reef risk.

A. Parametric Insurance

At its most basic, insurance is a risk management tool where the policy holder transfers risk from the owner or manager of an asset to the insurance provider. The insurance holder pays the premium to ensure funds when an insured asset is damaged or destroyed within the specifics the policy covers (Kousky and Light 2019). Insurance can increase the resilience of coral reefs by providing financial resources to restore and repair coral reefs after damage occurs.

The two main types of insurance are indemnity and parametric (Bergh et al. 2020, Wharton 2021). Indemnity insurance policies require a damage assessment to determine the severity of the damage sustained by an asset and the level of payout that will be provided based on the terms of the insurance policy. Since the assessment process can take months to complete, indemnity insurance may be a better option for ecosystems where rapid intervention following damage is not essential (Wharton 2021). Conversely, parametric insurance does not require a damage assessment, although proof of loss may be required depending on local insurance regulations. With parametric insurance, the payout, which is linked through a pre-agreed index to the intensity of the hazard causing the damage, can occur in a matter of days. Parametric insurance is most applicable when there is high value in having funds very quickly after a shock event so that the funds can immediately be deployed to moderate the impacts of the damage (Wharton 2021). Further, parametric insurance can cover contingent liability as well as direct damage, meaning that it has much broader potential usage, particularly given that natural assets in the marine environment are rarely "owned" in the same way as terrestrial physical assets.

---

[9] Global financial mechanisms include the Climate Investment Funds, the Green Climate Fund, the Adaptation Fund, the Global Environmental Facility, conservation trust funds, and national and regional development banks. National financial mechanisms may include policy options to collect and allocate funds to programs and projects designed to address specific issues (Lathan and Watkins 2020; United Nations Climate Change 2016; Meirovich, Peters, and Rios 2013).

For coral reefs, a parametric insurance product is likely to be the most appropriate in many cases given the effectiveness of rapid emergency restoration post damage (Zepeda et al. 2019). The rapid payout enables trained response brigades to quickly move to action, survey damage, develop restoration plans, and begin collecting and reattaching coral fragments to the main coral colony before they die, or transferring the fragments to nurseries for growth and transplanting later. Indeed, the world's first insurance policy on coral reefs was a parametric policy purchased in 2019 to cover the coral reef and beach in Quintana Roo, Mexico (Box 6).

Box 6

Parametric Insurance Policy in Quintana Roo, Mexico

Under the Trust for Coastal Zone Management, Social Development, and Security policy of 2018, Quintana Roo secures long-term private and public funding to manage coastal zones. It uses the policy for responding to emergencies and disaster events.

Starting in 2019, the trust bought a parametric insurance policy on behalf of the State of Quintana Roo and is the beneficiary of the policy. The trust renewed the parametric insurance policy in both 2020, 2021, and 2022. This policy has been modified from year to year, improving its design and payout structure.

The parametric insurance policy in Quintana Roo is triggered if wind speed within a predefined polygon is greater than 100 knots. Payouts are scaled with maximum recorded wind speed in the predefined polygon. At 100 knots, the payout is $850,000 and the maximum payout of $2.125 million is made when wind speeds exceed 160 knots.

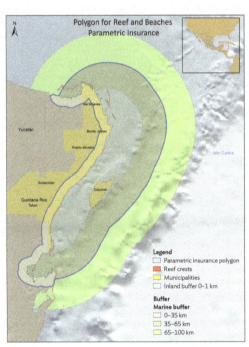

Predefined polygon for parametric insurance policy in Quintana Roo.

On 27 October 2020, the Quintana Roo Government announced that Hurricane Delta activated the insurance with wind speeds of 100 knots, triggering a payout of $850,000. In April 2021, the Trust Fund Board approved deploying the insurance payout in three major areas: (i) physical restoration of reefs damaged by Hurricane Delta and Hurricane Zeta; (ii) four projects, totaling $500,000 and implemented over 2 years, that include additional restoration work as well as training in building reef restoration capacity; and (iii) a reserve fund of $50,000 to cover response costs when the insurance is not triggered or, if triggered, to cover initial response activities before the payout is received. The board also approved purchase of the 2021 insurance policy with these funds, which helped offset pandemic-related drops in revenue. The trust paid $300,000 for the 2021 policy.

Source: The Nature Conservancy (2021a).

Generally, parametric insurance products are designed to pay a predetermined amount to the policyholder when specific and measurable event conditions, or parameters, occur in a defined geographic location. Predefined event conditions are characteristics of the event that can be correlated to the damages sustained by the coral reef and the resulting need for cash (Wharton 2021). Payouts are triggered by pre-agreed thresholds (e.g., peak wind speed greater than 64 knots) associated with the event condition. The conditions that trigger payouts must be objective measures collected independently by a third party, and the data on the conditions must be available quickly after the event.

Three types of parametric insurance policies are best suited to coral reefs—pure parametric, gridded parametric, and parametric index—as they best capture the relationship between hurricane intensity and reef response needs (Wharton 2021). The difference between these three types of policies is the method and resolution used to capture the spatial distribution and impacts of wind speed on the reef (Table 7) (Wharton 2021).

Table 7: Types of Parametric Insurance Structures for Coral Reefs

	Pure Parametric	Gridded Parametric	Parametric Index
Payout Structure	The payout is determined by the intensity of the hazard parameter in a defined geographic area ("polygon").	The payout is determined by the intensity of the hazard parameter in a defined geographic area, with that area divided into zones to which triggering thresholds are assigned. A zone closer to the coral reef could have a lower trigger threshold than one further away.	Builds on gridded parametric with payouts a function of spatial distribution of hazard parameter intensity, and spatial distribution of exposure/vulnerability used to estimate reef damage at a specific site. This involves calculating the spatial distribution of reef damage and then aggregating up to the site level to determine the payout amount.
Benefits	Simple, easy to understand and to communicate to stakeholders.	Captures spatial variation in the hazard intensity, with respect to the covered area. Remains relatively simple.	Capable of capturing various drivers of damage resulting in reduced basis risk.
Limitations	Higher basis risk, since the triggering event is relatively broadly defined and so not necessarily closely linked to the likely damage that may result.	Greater data requirements than a pure parametric, requires information on spatial distribution of reefs.	Greater data requirements than gridded parametric, requires information such as live coral cover which may not be available in all geographies. Depending on data availability, assumptions required around reef damage rates.
Currently in Place	Quintana Roo, Mexico.	Ten Mesoamerican Reef sites across Mexico, Belize, Guatemala, and Honduras. Three large sites across the State of Hawaii, United States.	Not currently in place.

Sources: Wharton (2021) and World Bank (2012).

In 2021, the Mesoamerican Reef Fund (MAR Fund), supported by the InsuResilience Solutions Fund and in collaboration with Willis Towers Watson (WTW), purchased a gridded parametric insurance policy to cover four pilot sites in the Mesoamerican Reef for the 2021 Atlantic hurricane season.[10] The four pilot reef sites—Banco Chinchorro, Arrecifes de Xcalak, Hol Chan, and Turneffe Atoll—directly protect more than 4,500 hectares of live coral cover and the insurance policy had an overall program limit of $2.5 million, with sublimits for each of the sites. For the gridded parametric policy, payouts at a given site are a function of wind speed and distance of observed wind speed from the protected site. For example, if a hurricane passes through Zone C with a maximum wind speed of 120 knots, the gridded parametric policy will pay out 40% of the site's limit (Figure 7). For the 2022 Atlantic hurricane season, three additional sites were added (Utila, Roatan and Guanaja, and Cabo Tres Puntas and Motaguilla), bringing the program to seven sites across four countries (Mexico, Belize, Honduras, and Guatemala).[11] The first ever payout of the policy, $175,000, was triggered by Hurricane Lisa in November 2022 at the Turneffe Atoll site off the coast of Belize (Mesoamerican Reef Fund 2022a). The MAR Fund program was further expanded on renewal in June 2023, with two sites added in Honduras and two sites added in Belize (Willis Towers Watson 2023).

Figure 7: Components of Parametric Insurance Policy for Mesoamerican Reef Site

A. Insurance Policy Payout Structure

Wind Speed (knots)	Zone A (purple)	Zone B (red)	Zone C (orange)	Zone D (green)
0 to 63	0%	0%	0%	0%
64 to 82	0%	0%	5%	10%
83 to 95	0%	5%	10%	20%
96 to 112	5%	10%	20%	40%
113 to 136	10%	20%	40%	80%
137 to more	20%	40%	80%	100%

B. Predefined Polygon

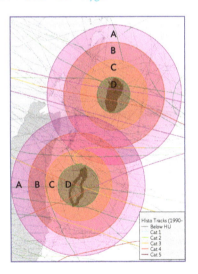

Source: Wharton 2021.

---

[10] The Mesoamerican Reef region lies within the Caribbean Sea and touches the coasts of Mexico, Belize, Guatemala, and Honduras. The InsuResilience Solutions Fund supports innovative solutions to mitigate negative impacts of climate change. InsuResilience Solutions Fund fosters the development of needs-based and financially sustainable climate risk insurance. As an implementing program of the InsuResilience Global Partnership, the fund is an important contribution of the German government funded by KfW Development Bank to achieve the targets of the international initiative on climate risk insurance "InsuResilience."

[11] The InsuResilience Solutions Fund will continue to provide financial support for insurance premiums covering the 2022 and 2023 Atlantic hurricane seasons. During this "proof-of-concept" phase, the MAR fund will consult and engage with the universe of reef users and beneficiaries—including MAR country governments (Belize, Guatemala, Honduras, and Mexico), local communities, tourists, and recreational users, businesses (e.g., in the tourism and fishing sectors), and global citizens—to develop and implement a sustainable long-term financing strategy.

More recently, The Nature Conservancy (TNC), supported by the Bank of America Charitable Foundation and the Howden Group Foundation, and in collaboration with WTW, purchased a gridded parametric insurance policy for three large sites covering all the main reef areas in the State of Hawaii for the 2022 and 2023 hurricane seasons (TNC 2022). Unlike the MAR Fund policy, this policy covers both hurricanes and tropical storms with windspeeds of at least 50 knots. The insurance policy has an overall program limit of $2 million with a sublimit of $1 million per site.

In these examples, coral reef insurance is designed to fund a rapid response to restore reefs damaged by a defined event, such as a tropical cyclone. Coral reef insurance has not been designed to directly pay out to individuals that rely on the reef, such as for tourism income, fishing income, or to reimburse them for other business loss incurred by the damage. Instead, these individuals who rely on reef services benefit from the coral reef insurance and post-storm restoration efforts to support and maintain the health of the coral reef (WTW and MAR Fund 2019).

B. Other Innovative Financing Instruments

In addition to insurance, other innovative funding sources can be used alone or in conjunction with other sources to manage a portfolio of risks to coral reefs. A range of these additional funding sources are described below. Although the list is not exhaustive, it does provide an idea of the broad range of financial tools available to fund coral reef management, restoration, and post-disaster repair.

> **Resilience insurance:** Resilience insurance incentivizes pre-disaster investment in coral reef restoration by promising a discount on the insurance premiums of standard policies covering onshore infrastructure (Reguero et al. 2020). The premium savings, which are calculated based on the amount of flood protection benefits to the onshore infrastructure provided by the restored reef, amortize part of the upfront cost of reef restoration. Resilience insurance is best suited for reefs that require both immediate restoration and ongoing management to establish and maintain the reef's resilience capacity (Bergh et al. 2020, Reguero 2020). The resilience insurance concept has not yet been deployed for coral reefs but has been assessed for wildfire and riverine flood resilience (Martinez et al. 2021, TNC 2021b). Conservation International is piloting a multi-faceted approach, via a specially established social enterprise called the Restoration Insurance Service Company, in which coastal asset owners could receive discounted insurance premiums due to the verified flood risk reduction benefits provided by mangroves (The Lab 2022).
>
> **Insurance-linked securities:** Insurance-linked securities are financial instruments utilized to transfer risk to capital market investors (Climate Bonds Initiative 2019). Their underlying value is contingent on an insurance related event, usually one of low-frequency but high-severity (Climate Bonds Initiative 2019). Catastrophe bonds and resilience bonds are types of insurance-linked securities.
>
> > **Catastrophe bonds:** With a catastrophe bond, capital market investors would provide funds through a special purpose vehicle to pay for post-damage coral reef restoration costs should a disaster event due to a specified natural hazard occur (Climate Bonds

Initiative 2019, Iyer et al. 2018). If the disaster event does not occur over the term of the bond, investors receive both principal and interest. If the event does occur, the investors receive only the interest, with the principal (or a portion of it) used to cover post-damage coral reef restoration (Iyer et al. 2018). Typically, institutional investors are incentivized to invest in catastrophe bonds as a way to achieve environmental, social, and governance goals while also diversifying their investment portfolio and potentially earning a return (Evans 2021). Historically, catastrophe bonds have been issued for disaster events with an annual probability of occurrence of 2% or less (World Bank 2012). Most frequently, catastrophe bonds are issued by insurance companies, reinsurers, and state catastrophe funds.

Resilience bonds: Resilience bonds, in essence, are a variation of catastrophe bonds. Within the insurance industry, the term refers to a combination of a debt instrument, such as a loan, combined with a risk transfer mechanism, such as an insurance policy. A fundamental principle behind resilience bonds is that investments in resilience will, for example, reduce the risk of default on the loan and reduce the risk of damage or loss of the insured asset. As a part of the resilience bond, the insured party receives insurance savings that are directed to an ex-ante resilience intervention (e.g., reef restoration prior to a disaster event to improve the reef's resilience to a disaster event).[12] By construction, resilience bonds emphasize exposure to climate hazards (Climate Bonds Initiative 2019). Although the concept of the resilience bond was established in 2015, the approach has yet to gain widespread adoption due to challenges with modeling and timing differences between resilience projects and bond payback periods (Muir 2022).

Regional risk pools: In regional risk pools, participating entities, which are often country governments, purchase insurance coverage against a natural hazard as a group (Deutz, Kellet, and Zoltani 2018). By collectively purchasing the insurance, the risk of a disaster event occurring is spread across all entities, which lowers the premium cost that any individual entity would be charged if they purchased the insurance on their own. Smaller entities or entities in high-risk areas may be able to purchase insurance coverage through regional risk pools that, without the premium savings, would be too expensive to consider (ADB 2020a). In addition to purchasing insurance at a reduced rate as a group, regional risk pools can also provide participating entities with tools to enhance disaster risk assessment and capacity building to facilitate planning and response activities. The Caribbean Catastrophe Risk Insurance Facility, the first regional risk pool established in 2007, provided parametric insurance coverage for earthquakes, hurricanes, and extreme rainfall events to participating Caribbean countries (currently 23). Today, there is also a Pacific Catastrophe Risk Insurance Company and an African Risk Capacity.[13]

---

[12] This definition of resilience bonds differs from the one used in the green bond market, which uses the term to more generally refer to bonds which use proceeds to support climate resilience (Climate Bonds Initiative 2019).

[13] The Pacific Catastrophe Risk Insurance Company (PCRIC) is a captive insurance company, a form of self-insurance, that is owned by Pacific island nations. PCRIC uses parametric insurance policies to help increase Pacific island nations' capacity to meet immediate post-disaster needs. Current member countries include Cook Islands, Fiji, the Marshall Islands, Samoa, Tonga, and Vanuatu, with nine additional countries eligible to become members. For more information, see https://pcric.org/.

Emergency fund: These are funds set aside from an entity's reserves to address unforeseen circumstances, essentially acting as a self-insurance mechanism. In relation to coral reef risk management, emergency funds can be used to implement response activities after a disaster event causes damage to a reef, but the event does not trigger an insurance payout. After Hurricane Delta triggered an insurance payout in October 2020 in Quintana Roo, Mexico, the Coastal Zone Management Trust used a portion of the insurance payout to establish an emergency fund for this purpose (Box 6). The MAR Fund also operates an emergency fund (Box 7). In Asia and the Pacific, ADB introduced its own contingent disaster financing in 2019 to support its members in disaster preparedness and post-disaster relief (ADB 2019).

Box 7

Emergency Fund for the Mesoamerican Reef Fund

The Mesoamerican Reef Fund (MAR Fund) established an emergency fund to provide immediate and timely funding to coral reefs affected by disaster events due to natural hazards or human activities. The emergency fund strengthens the resilience and adaptive abilities of coastal marine areas in the Mesoamerican Reef (MAR), especially affected coral reefs. The emergency fund was created in 2017 and is capitalized annually with funds from the return rate of the endowment granted by KfW (Kreditanstalt für Wiederaufbau), a German state-owned investment and development bank. In addition, the emergency fund is the primary mechanism for the payout management of the parametric insurance policy purchased by MAR Fund.

Through the emergency fund, the MAR Fund allocates funds to response teams with the capacity (training and equipment) to respond to an eligible emergency. For the emergency fund, an eligible emergency can be (i) natural hazards, such as cyclones, hurricanes, and storms; (ii) vessel groundings; (iii) damage caused by different nautical devices (e.g., anchors, buoys); and (iv) other types of damage that emergency funds can address. The emergency fund can be used in coral reef areas of the four MAR countries—Belize, Guatemala, Honduras, and Mexico—and the maximum amount for a request for immediate response is $25,000, although more total funds could be paid out if the insurance policy is triggered.

Emergency funds are distributed to response teams through local organizations that meet the eligibility requirements. The local organization is then in charge of procuring the supplies, resources, and necessary assistance for response teams to immediately address the emergency or disaster for which the funding was requested. Eligible funding recipients are nongovernment organizations with administrative mechanisms to manage grant funding promptly and effectively at the time of an emergency. Eligible funding recipients are not required to be a part of a response team, yet they must have a working relationship with these teams and be committed to working together to address the emergency.

Source: MAR (2022b).

Blue bonds and green bonds: Broadly, bonds, which are a type of fixed-income instrument, are a form of tradable debt established when the investor loans money to the bond issuer, which is usually a government or company, who promises to repay the loan plus interest on an agreed schedule (Victurine et al. 2022). With green bonds, the financing is directed toward projects that have environmental benefits, and with blue bonds, a subset of green bonds, the financing is directed toward blue economy projects, such as coral reef restoration.[14] Some green bonds may be marketed as "resilience bonds" due to the types of projects they finance. However, they may not include the risk transfer element specific to resilience bonds as defined by the insurance industry. An example of a green bond is the idea for a Pacific Ocean Resilience Bond, which would finance resilient infrastructure and positively benefit marine biodiversity and productivity (Tuivuniwai 2021).

Debt-for-nature swaps: Debt-for-nature swaps (or debt relief mechanisms) allow a portion of a country's foreign debt to be forgiven in exchange for commitments to invest in biodiversity conservation and environmental policy measures (Victurine et al. 2022). Restructuring debt in tandem with blue bond financing can generate significant capital for coral reef conservation while also reducing a country's debt, lowering interest rates, and/or extending debt repayment periods. For example, the United States government, through its Tropical Forest and Coral Reefs Conservation Act, and TNC, through its Blue Bonds for Ocean Conservation program, in addition to other actors, work with countries to refinance a portion of their debt as green or blue bonds (Victurine et al. 2022). In 2021, TNC announced a $364 million transaction with the Government of Belize that generated approximately $180 million for marine conservation (TNC 2021c). The transaction included the world's first "catastrophe wrapper," a parametric insurance policy that provides insurance to cover loan repayments following eligible hurricane events (WTW 2021). To date, ADB has not been involved in similar debt restructuring efforts.

Blue carbon credits: Blue carbon refers to the ability of coastal and marine environments such as mangroves, salt marshes, and sea grasses to sequester and store carbon dioxide from the atmosphere. Blue carbon credits monetize the carbon capture abilities of these coastal ecosystems by selling the carbon credits to buyers as a means of compensating the buyers' carbon emissions (ADB 2022). The funding raised via the sale of the blue carbon credits can be used to finance the restoration of coastal ecosystems. Blue carbon credits could be combined with resilience credits.

Resilience credits: In 2018, TNC announced the development of a combined blue carbon and resilience credit to value coastal wetlands' ability to store carbon and increase resilience of coastal communities. The credits will be certified by Verra, an independent third party, and be based on their carbon value and resilience benefits. This novel instrument will enable investors to offset carbon emissions and support increased coastal resilience simultaneously. The first blue carbon and resilience credits are expected to be available in 2023. More broadly, at this stage, resilience credits do not have a clear market as ambiguity remains around what could be done by a buyer with a credit, in addition to limited willingness to pay for such a credit.

---

[14] The Biodiversity Finance Initiative. 2022. BIOFIN Catalogue of Finance Solutions (accessed 21 September 2022).

Blended finance: Blended finance is defined as the strategic use of development funds from government and philanthropic sources to mobilize private capital for social and environmental outcomes (Victurine et al. 2022). With blended finance, public and private resources are pooled to create more attractive investment opportunities, that is, investments that are easy monetizable or less risky. Blended finance structures can vary and may utilize several financial instruments in tandem, though an overarching goal for this structuring approach is to de-risk investment opportunities to attract private sector investment, which will require an economically viable business model. Examples of blended finance in action include the Global Fund for Coral Reefs and the Seychelles Blue Bond (Victurine et al. 2022).

Any given funding source will be best suited to finance a particular component of reef restoration and repair work. In most instances, multiple instruments will be needed to adequately finance reef management, reef restoration, and post-disaster reef repair (Table 8).

Table 8: Innovative Funding Sources for Reef Management, Restoration, and Repair

Funding Source	Ongoing Reef Management	Restoration of Degraded Reefs	Post-Disaster Reef Repair
Parametric insurance			√
Resilience insurance	√	√	
Catastrophe bonds			√
Resilience bonds	√	√	
Regional risk pools			√
Emergency fund			√
Blue bonds and green bonds[a]	√	√	
Debt-for-nature swaps[a]	√	√	
Blue carbon credits[a]	√	√	
Resilience credits[a]	√	√	
Blended finance[a]	√	√	

[a] These funding sources should include emergency fund as a part of setup.
Source: The Nature Conservancy.

In addition, any innovative funding source that relies on the open market will require clear data and evidence of (i) the exact uses of the funds provided by the innovative funding source, (ii) the entity or entities who will hold the financing on their balance sheets, and (iii) the mechanisms to repay the finances as well as the parties liable for the repayment. That is, once a possible funding source is identified it may still take months to years to gather the data and evidence needed to bring it realization.

VI

A POST-DAMAGE RESPONSE MECHANISM TO IMPLEMENT AN EFFECTIVE FINANCIAL SCHEME

As noted, tropical storms and other events can inflict considerable damage on coral reefs by reducing live coral cover and structural complexity. Addressing the damage quickly and effectively is critical to reducing damage to affected corals and for increasing the likelihood that reefs will continue to provide valuable services to local communities in the future.

Repairing reefs, however, can be costly. The restoration of coral reefs is rarely a governmental priority in the aftermath of extreme events, as resources are focused on life-saving actions and the reconstruction of grey infrastructure and property. Consequently, the post-disaster restoration of coral reefs is spread across reef users, without any clearly defined institutional process to organize and fund the response.[15] As noted in the previous section, coral reef insurance, in addition to other financial schemes, is one innovative way of closing this funding gap and developing a clear and actionable process for repairing coral reefs post storm.

Throughout, this section discusses the response mechanism and corresponding institutional arrangement that can be created to effectively repair damage to a coral reef following a disaster event. The post-disaster response mechanism outlines who and how coral reefs will be repaired following the disaster event, such as a tropical storm, while the institutional arrangement outlines who and how the post-disaster response will be funded. This post-disaster response can be funded with many of the innovative funding sources described above (Table 8). Coral reef insurance should be purchased only if the post-disaster response capacity is already established.

---

[15] Funds are primarily needed to purchase materials and tools, fuel, diving gear rental, boat rental, and, when necessary, vehicle rental. Funds can also be used to train coral reef first responders and for other operational needs.

A. Post-Damage Response Mechanism

The response mechanism is comprised of an organizational and operational structure. The organizational and operational structure determines roles, responsibilities, and information flows between the different levels of response coordination. The preferred structure is composed of a lead agency, a coordination committee, an operations team, an on-the-ground response team, and a support network (Table 9). However, the structure should be flexible, consider the diversity of actors involved, and fit the resources available.

Table 9: Key Components of Post-Storm Response Mechanism

Component	Description
Lead agency	Creates all governance bodies, leads the coordination committee, and ensures that the managers of protected areas organize and maintain an emergency response plan.
Coordination committee	Tailors the structure and implementation of the response protocol to local needs, manages funds to implement response activities, and coordinates all the activities of the response. The coordinating committee is composed of stakeholders from key institutions committed to the response capacity and involved in the management of protected areas. Members are normally (but not exclusively) staff of the national government, protected natural area managers, local nongovernment organizations, and leaders of community groups or private sector.
Operations team	Coordinates the logistics and communications needed for the implementation of the response, including supplying materials and establishing partnerships with key institutions and companies to procure supplies and a place to operate. This team can be composed of any member of the community who wants to support the response efforts but is not part of the reef brigade team.
Reef brigades	Consists of on-the-ground teams of experienced and well-trained divers, snorkelers and support staff who conduct in-the-water response, directly cleaning and repairing the reefs. This team can include local community members such as fishers and tourism operators. It is highly recommended that members of this team reside close to where the response will be implemented.
Support network	A network of partner organizations that provides necessary resources and staff for the response. The support network can include key partners such as government agencies, private sector (tour operators, restaurants, gas stations, etc.), nongovernment organizations, reef managers, universities, fishers, and others looking to contribute to response efforts.

Source: The Nature Conservancy.

B. Institutional Arrangement to Buy and Manage a Coral Reef Insurance Policy

Many stakeholders may be involved in the institutional arrangement supporting the insurance policy, depending on the complexity of their interests, regulatory environment, and ownership of the coral reefs. The institutional arrangement can vary from a single entity, as the owner of the asset who buys the insurance policy and implements the post-storm response, to a complex one. Table 10 identifies the primary elements of the institutional arrangement. Ultimately, insurance policy payouts will only be effective if they are managed within a clear institutional structure and if stakeholders have access to the technical and human capacities, the equipment, and the resources needed to respond after a tropical storm. To make sure this institutional structure is in place, a concerted effort around capacity building may be needed prior to purchase of a coral reef insurance policy.

Table 10: Institutional Arrangements to Implement Coral Reef Insurance Policy

Element	Description
Who finances the insurance premium	Ideally, the entities legally responsible for the care of the coral reefs or those who receive ecosystem service benefits from the coral reef will finance the insurance premium. In the absence of interest or ability from these groups to finance the premium, other willing organizations or groups may choose to provide funds to cover the purchase of the premium. Innovative approaches may also be utilized to raise funds (e.g., green fees for tourism).
Who purchases the insurance policy	National laws define who can buy an insurance policy. The entity buying the insurance policy—known as the "named insured"—must have an insurable interest, legal authority, and financial capacity. Typically, the entities legally responsible for the care of the coral reefs, or those who receive benefits from the ecosystem service, are legally allowed to buy and pay for the insurance policy. The entity must also have strong governance and administration, and relationships, processes, and protocols already established to distribute predictable and timely funds for coral reef response. It is critical to conduct a legal assessment to review all insurance regulations.
Who receives the insurance payout	The entity that will receive the insurance payout must have the capacity to manage the funds with transparency and accountability to all stakeholders and ensure that the funds are used for their intended purpose. The recipient of the insurance payout does not need to be the same entity as the financer or purchaser of the insurance policy; if local insurance regulations permit, third parties could receive the insurance payout.
Governance and process to manage insurance payout	A governance process defines the procedures to decide on the use of the insurance payout, including how restoration projects will be approved, funded, and monitored. The coordination committee must be directly involved in the governance and the process to manage the payout.

Source: Fajardo, McLeod, and Tassoulas 2019.

C. Example: Parametric Insurance Policy in Quintano Roo, Mexico

In Quintana Roo, the Technical Committee (a board of directors) manages the Trust for Coastal Zone Management, Social Development, and Security (see Box 6), with representation from the State of Quintana Roo, local municipalities, hotel associations, nongovernment organizations, as well as the secretaries of the environment, tourism, finance and planning, public safety, and social development. Each of the two subcommittees—the Coastal Zone Management Subcommittee and the Social Development and Security Subcommittee—has an advisory council that draws on member expertise to advise the subcommittee and the Technical Committee in decision-making. Coastal and marine experts from the Coastal Zone Advisory Council, for example, guide reef repair and restoration. The trust is funded through a range of contributions and uses the money to pay ongoing reef maintenance, an emergency, the premium for the parametric insurance coverage (Figure 8).

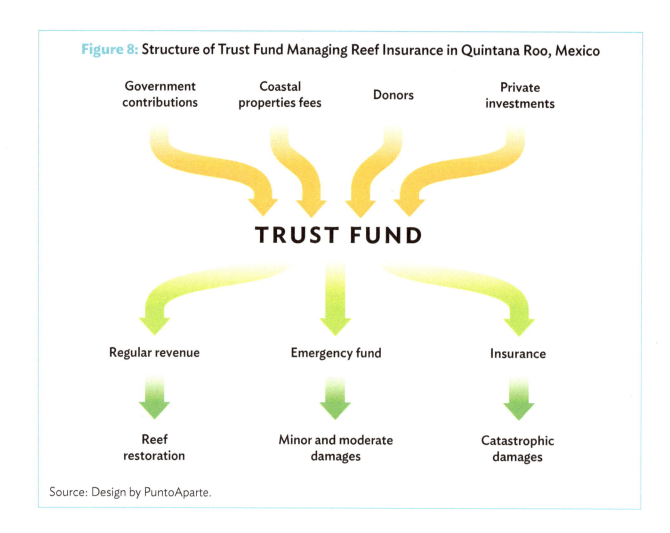

Figure 8: Structure of Trust Fund Managing Reef Insurance in Quintana Roo, Mexico

Source: Design by PuntoAparte.

To ensure capacity for timely and effective post-storm restoration, six reef brigades, consisting of 60 people, were trained between 2018 and 2019.[16] Since the training, the reef brigades have performed rescue activities in response to tropical storms and ship groundings and, in 2020, performed post-storm restoration activities following damage from three tropical storms and the activation of the parametric insurance coverage.[17]

Following the impact of Hurricane Delta, staff of the National Commission of Protected Areas and Fisheries Research Institute, Puerto Morelos campus, conducted a rapid assessment of reef damage in several areas of coral reef in the Puerto Morelos, Cancun, and Isla Mujeres marine protected areas. The reef brigades—made up of 53 community members, many of them tour operators—implemented needed response actions identified through the assessments from October 2021 to January 2021.[18] For example, the reef brigades working in the Puerto Morelos Reef National Park stabilized 1,933 coral colonies displaced or overturned by storm surge and rescued and transplanted nearly 12,000 broken coral fragments. The reef brigades working in Punta Cancun, Punta Nizuc, and the West Coast of Isla Mujeres Reefs National Park stabilized 38 coral colonies and transplanted nearly 350 broken coral fragments.

D. Example: Parametric Insurance Policy in Mesoamerican Reef

The Mesoamerican Reef Insurance Program, covering seven sites across the Mesoamerican Reef (see section V) utilizes an emergency fund for the collection and disbursal of insurance payouts following the occurrence of a qualifying hurricane. The payout is intended to be made within days of the qualifying event. Local nongovernment organizations at the affected reef sites are transferring funds from the emergency fund—based on a pre-agreed process—to implement post-storm restoration protocols (Box 7).

To build up capacity for these post-storm restoration efforts, The Nature Conservancy (TNC) and MAR Fund, in collaboration with the national governments of Belize, Honduras, and Mexico, trained reef brigades in Northern Belize (40 people), Bay Islands and Tela in Honduras (50 people), and in Banco Chinchorro and Xcalak in Mexico (20 people). In addition, they develop post-storm response governance and response plans in each of the countries (Table 11).

---

[16] Brigades were trained by TNC in collaboration with the National Commission of Protected Areas, the State Government of Quintana Roo, and the Center for Research on Aquaculture and Fisheries. The training took place at three different sites within Quintana Roo—Puerto Morelos, Isla Mujeres, and Cancun.

[17] Three tropical cyclones damaged coral reefs in Quintana Roo in less than a month: Tropical Storm Gamma (3–5 October), Hurricane Delta (7 October), and Hurricane Zeta (27 October). Hurricane Delta made landfall with windspeeds in excess of 100 knots, which triggered an insurance payout of roughly $850,000 (Box 4).

[18] The reef brigades were funded by an emergency fund ($18,000) established by the Reef Rescue Initiative, TNC ($3,000), and local in-kind contributions (gas, boats, diving services, food, and volunteers).

Following Hurricane Lisa in November 2022, which triggered the first ever payout of by the MAR Insurance Programme, the two insurance underwriters, AXA Climate and Munich Re, transferred the $175,000 to the emergency fund within 12 days. MAR Fund was then able to rapidly distribute resources to support emergency reef restoration of the Turneffe Atoll site, conducted by specially trained brigades, which are governed and coordinated by the Fisheries Department and the Turneffe Atoll Sustainability Association in Belize. These brigades will implement the pre-agreed local reef response plan, beginning with a rapid damage assessment and cleanup, followed by rehabilitation and repair efforts.

Table 11: Governance Structure in Mexico, Belize, Honduras, and Guatemala

Country	Description
Mexico	The leading entity, National Commission of Protected Areas, with the approval of the advisory committee in each of the marine protected areas, formed the coordinating committee with its respective governance structure. Each marine protected area has an independent coordinating committee.
Belize	The lead entity, Belize Fisheries Department, formed the coordinating committee with its respective governance structure. That structure includes a brigade leader and operations team for each administrative region into which the country is divided: North, Central, and South.
Honduras	The lead entity, Instituto de Conservación Forestal, Áreas Protegidas y Vida Silvestre, with the approval of the Co-management Committee in each marine protected area, formed three coordinating committees, one for each of the marine protected areas with reefs in the Caribbean: Bay Islands, Cayos Cochinos, and Tela.
Guatemala	In development. The coordination committee was formed in November 2022 and will receive training on the protocol and response plan before establishing governance structure.

Source: Information in table compiled by The Nature Conservancy.

VII

IDENTIFYING OPPORTUNITIES FOR CORAL REEF INSURANCE IN ASIA AND THE PACIFIC

Across Asia and the Pacific, there are likely many places where an insurance policy could be a cost-effective way—that is, the price of the premium payments is offset by the protective value provided by the coral reefs—to ensure funds are available to restore coral reefs following triggering events. Identifying specific sites where such an insurance policy could be launched, however, requires detailed knowledge of various sites and local characteristics. Table 12 lays out essential questions when determining if a coral reef insurance policy is appropriate.

Table 12: Key Components of an Insurance Scheme for Post-Storm Response

Criteria	Description
Is insurance a viable option to support reef recovery?	
Coral reefs provide a valuable service to people and the economy.	A specific coral reef site may protect coastal assets and populations from flooding, sustain fisheries, or serve as key tourist attraction. Ideally, these benefits can be quantified in economic terms. Coral reefs also have well-recognized biodiversity value, even though it is more difficult to estimate in economic terms.
The services provided by coral reefs are diminished by the occurrence of an insurable hazard.	In the context of a coral reef insurance policy, the insurable hazard must occur randomly. There also must be enough information on the impact of the hazard on coral reefs to make pricing and underwriting possible.[a] The hazards most likely to satisfy these criteria include tropical cyclones, climate and ocean change, stormwater runoff, and tsunamis.[b]
The cost of repairing the reef damage is less than the losses in service provision.	To establish a business case for the insurance policy, the estimated costs for repairing coral reef damage after the occurrence of the insured hazard must be less than the estimated losses to the economy and people if the coral reefs were not repaired.

continued on next page

Table 12: *Continued*

Criteria	Description
Are there potential buyers of the coral reef insurance policy?	
The beneficiaries and/or parties responsible for managing the coral reefs are interested in restoring the damages.	Interested parties must recognize that coral reefs provide sufficient value to them that it is worth investing in repairing the damage to coral reefs. Beneficiaries may be informed by economic data, but decisions also may be influenced by cultural views and political perspectives.
The beneficiaries have the capacity to pay for an insurance premium.	The beneficiaries will be most interested in an insurance policy when post-damage response costs exceed their financial capacity to fund the repair. Constant annual premium costs may be easier to financially manage than unpredictable and large post-damage response costs. Reasonable estimates for the insurance premium are between 8% and 16% of the maximum payout.[c]
The beneficiaries are entitled to buy a coral reef insurance policy.	National and local law may dictate which parties and organizations are eligible to purchase an insurance policy. Given that regulations apply nationally, they do not influence site selection if the selection is within the country.

[a] Kousky and Light 2019 (355).
[b] Bergh et al. 2020 (22–23).
[c] Fajardo, McLeod, and Tassoulas 2019 (11).
Source: Information in table compiled by The Nature Conservancy.

Answering the first two questions may be based on available information and existing appreciation from stakeholders or can be fully assessed using economic data and damage models. For example, the protective value of coral reef ecosystems can be modeled by combining oceanographic data, including local topographic and bathymetric data and running hydrodynamic, waves and morphodynamicsmodels, to estimate flood and coastal erosion damages to coastal communities with and without coral reefs.[19]

In particular, a reef damage model is helpful to model the potential damage to reefs from the specific natural hazard risk that is being insured against. For example, in the context of tropical cyclones, wind speed has been shown to be one of the storm characteristics that best predicts coral reef damage, albeit with a wide range of variability.[20] A specific coral reef site's exposure and vulnerability to damage from tropical cyclones could be informed by site-specific data such as the spatial extent of live coral cover and the coral reef site's location relative to the dominant direction of the storm approach (e.g., leeward or windward).[21] The output of a reef damage model shows the anticipated number of hectares of coral reef at a specific site likely to be damaged by a tropical cyclone of varying wind speeds.[22]

---

[19] This approach is often referred to as the expected damage function, or damage cost avoided (Beck et al. 2018).

[20] For insurance models, the event causing the coral reef damage, in this case wind generated from tropical cyclones, is known as the hazard. The International Best Track Archive for Climate Stewardship (IBTrACS) provides data on the location and intensity of global tropical cyclones (Pérez-Cervantes et al. 2020).

[21] While coral reef cover data may be available from global data sets, field investigations can be required to determine the percent of live coral cover at a specific site (Pérez-Cervantes et al. 2020).

[22] The relationship between the hazard, i.e., wind speed, and coral reef damage is known as a fragility curve in the insurance industry.

By aggregating the total area of damaged coral for the covered geography and linking the area to reef response costs, the output can be converted to a monetary value and used to determine insurance payout amounts.

In addition, other elements will be important for designing the insurance policy and post-disaster response. These include:

> **The condition of the coral reef:** The single most important variable that predicts the extent of storm damage is live coral cover (Pérez-Cervantes et al. 2020). The best preserved sites are more likely to be severely impacted than degraded sites. In addition, beneficiaries may have more interest in repairing damage to coral reefs when the coral reef is in a healthy and undamaged state. In reality, many coral reefs that provide substantial value to inland communities are already disturbed. The coral reefs do not need to be in a good condition to be cost-effective to protect with an insurance policy to cover post-disaster response but, at the same time, the most heavily degraded reefs will likely not be cost-effective to protect with such policies.

> **The strength and existing capacity to repair and address the damages:** The gap between the existing capacity and that needed to implement a meaningful post-disaster response will be considered in policy design. Insurance would be considered non-viable only if it is not possible to build the full capacity needed to repair the damage. In addition, it is helpful to consider if there are competing hazards and threats to the coral reef that also may impact the coral reefs' ability to recover post damage.

The ultimate price of an insurance policy will be influenced by many factors and, at the time of purchase, is an estimate of the true cost of the policy (Onofrietti 2022). In addition to many of the local site-specific factors described above (e.g., location of coral reef, post-storm response costs), global factors, such as the cost of reinsurance protection (local insurers purchase reinsurance to protect their overall portfolio of assets), the operating costs of the insurer offering the policy, and trends in the global economy, can all influence the policy price (Onofrietti 2022). Other factors inherent to the structure of the policy, such as per-site payout limits and/or the aggregate policy limit (also known as the maximum payout that could be received during the policy period) will influence the price of the insurance premium. The amount of funding the purchaser has available for insurance premium payments can also influence the amount of coverage purchased. The insurance purchaser will need to decide how much financial risk to transfer via the insurance or via other financial schemes, such as an emergency fund.

The following reviews specific locations and regions in Asia and the Pacific where it may be possible to protect coral reefs with an insurance policy. That is, these sites pass many of the initial criteria listed in Table 10 and now require further exploration around the specifics and viability of a coral reef insurance policy.

A. Site-Specific Opportunities in Indonesia, the Philippines, Solomon Islands, and Fiji

Fiji, Indonesia, the Philippines, and the Solomon Islands are four countries where an insurance scheme may be possible. Policy and regulatory frameworks within these countries codify ocean protection and/or specifically recognize coral reefs and marine habitats more widely as opportunities to advance nature-based solutions within their nationally determined contributions (Carmago 2022a). The initial review of these four countries, while promising, focused primarily on the favorability of the institutional and governance structure. Further work remains in understanding the viability of a policy in these locations that promotes biodiversity through the financing of nature-based solutions including de-risking instruments, sufficient funding for premium payments and cost-effectiveness of these payments relative to other options. More information about each of the countries, as well as specific potential sites within them, is provided as follows.

Indonesia

Indonesia's coral reefs are about 16% of the world's and are the second largest of any nation globally (Yayasan Konservasi Alam Nustantara [YKAN] 2021). An initial analysis identified seven sites for their potential to advance a coral reef insurance scheme (Figure 9).

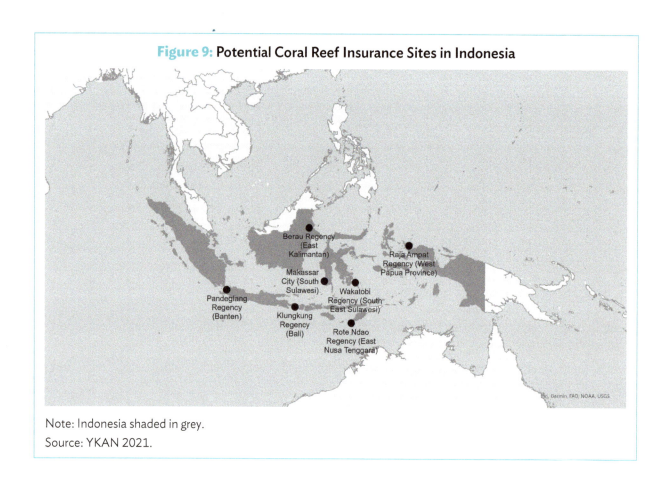

Figure 9: Potential Coral Reef Insurance Sites in Indonesia

Note: Indonesia shaded in grey.
Source: YKAN 2021.

About 60% of Indonesia's population lives along the coast and nearly one-third of it relies on nearshore fisheries for livelihoods. A 2016 study shows that coral reefs in the country would protect nearly 1.8 million people during a 100-year storm event (Spalding, Brumbaugh, and Landis 2016). In built infrastructure, other studies estimate that the country's coral reefs avert between $450 million and $639 million worth of damage annually from storms (Beck et al. 2018; Spalding, Brumbaugh, and Landis 2016). In addition, the tourism, recreation, and fisheries sector all benefit from the presence of coral reef ecosystems (Camargo 2022a). Some coral reefs in Indonesia generate over $1 million in tourism revenue annually and the annual value of reef-associated tourism across Indonesia exceeds $3 billion (YKAN 2021). Finally, the country's marine fisheries and aquaculture sectors have been valued at $14 billion and $7 billion, respectively (YKAN 2021).

Coral reefs across Indonesia are threatened by many potentially insurable risks, including strong winds, high tides and storm surge, intense rainfall, tropical cyclones, marine heatwaves and cold-water anomalies, tsunamis, volcanic eruption, and earthquakes (YKAN 2021, Camargo 2022a). While additional assessments are needed to understand how coral reefs at these seven sites are damaged by disaster events, post-hazard damages have been documented. For example, after the Lombok earthquake of 2018, broken corals were identified on reef sites and adjacent beaches and high sediment concentrations were observed on the reefs around Klungkung Regency (YKAN 2021). Changes in sea surface temperature, which may become more frequent with climate change, have bleached corals in Indonesia, and have severely impacted reefs near Makassar and Klungkun (YKAN 2021). More recently, in April 2021, impacts on coral reefs were observed near Rote Ndao Regency after Tropical Cyclone Seroja (GEF 2021).

Across these seven sites, stakeholders are interested in both marine conservation and protection and disaster risk reduction; however, perceptions of risk and how to manage it differ across the sites (YKAN 2021). For example, in Pandeglang and Makassar, where stakeholders observed the damages caused by the Sundra Strait Tsunami, stakeholders prioritized coral reef restoration after damage from natural hazard events. In Raja Ampat and Wakatobi, stakeholders viewed human activities and climate change as the biggest threats to coral reefs (YKAN 2021).

Finally, government agencies and some private sector actors in Indonesia have considered insurance within a broader disaster risk financing framework (Camargo 2022a). The Financial Services Authority is the main regulator of insurance and financial products in Indonesia (YKAN 2021). National insurance companies in Indonesia have also formed an Indonesia-based reinsurance agency, Maipark (YKAN 2021). The Ministry of Finance is also currently establishing a trust fund for disaster insurance for government infrastructure.[23] In addition, several other trust funds have been established, including the Central Trust fund used for management of environmental funds, and the Indonesia Climate Change Trust Fund used for management of funds from the World Bank and Global Environment Facility for coral reef management (YKAN 2021).

---

[23] Presidential Decree No. 80 of 2011 enables the establishment of trust funds, and requires that they have a board of trustees and trust fund managers (YKAN 2021).

Table 13 summarizes the key characteristics of these seven sites in Indonesia related to their feasibility for the development of a coral reef insurance policy.

Table 13: Key Characteristics of Seven Potential Sites for an Insurance Policy in Indonesia

	Berau	Klungkung	Makassar	Pandeglang	Raja Ampat	Rote Ndao	Wakatobi
1. Coral reefs provide a valuable service to people and the economy.							
Population living less than 10 meters above sea level and within 10 kilometers of a coral reef.[a]	16,615	56,499	1,363,893	83,247	14,583	29,814	60,986
Tourism value of direct uses and indirect uses of coral reefs ($ million per year).[b]	$33.55	$2.93	$28.80	$36.76	$27.46	$14.83	$15.89
2. Services provided by coral reefs are diminished by the occurrence of an insurable hazard.							
Earthquakes[c]		Yes		Yes			
Marine heatwaves	Yes	Yes	Yes	Yes	Yes	Yes	
Tropical cyclones[d]		Yes		Yes		Yes	
Tsunamis[e]	Yes	Yes		Yes	Yes	Yes	
Volcanic eruptions		Yes		Yes			
3. The cost of repairing the reef damage is less than the losses in service provision.							
	Additional assessment required.						
4. The beneficiaries and/or parties responsible for managing the coral reefs are interested in restoring the damages.							
	Many, but not all, of Indonesia's reefs are found in designated conservation areas and managed by federal ministries or provincial governments. There is strong recognition of the need to establish financial scheme to fund post-disaster coral reef restoration at both the national and site level.[f]						
5. The beneficiaries have the capacity to pay for an insurance premium.							
	Financial capacity is low at the city and regency level; however, it may be possible to raise funds from private corporate social responsibility initiatives.[g]						
6. The beneficiaries are entitled to buy a coral reef insurance policy.							
	Additional assessment required but based on preliminary assessment, Indonesian insurance market appears sufficiently well-organized and regulated.[h]						

[a] YKAN 2021.
[b] Direct uses include coral reef based fisheries, aquaculture, reef mining, and tourism, while indirect uses include coastal protection, carbon sequestration, option value, existence value, and bequest value (GEF 2021).
[c] YKAN 2021, Figure 4.
[d] YKAN 2021, Figure 3.
[e] YKAN 2021, Figure 5.
[f] YKAN 2021.
[g] YKAN 2021.
[h] Camargo 2022a.

Philippines

With about 26,000 square kilometers of coral reef, the Philippines is home to the third-largest reef system in the world (Roa-Quiaoit 2021). The country was identified as a top-tier candidate to explore potential to develop an insurance scheme as part of an overarching risk management and sustainable funding strategy for coral reef protection and conservation, in particular around six sites (Figure 10) (Camargo 2022a).

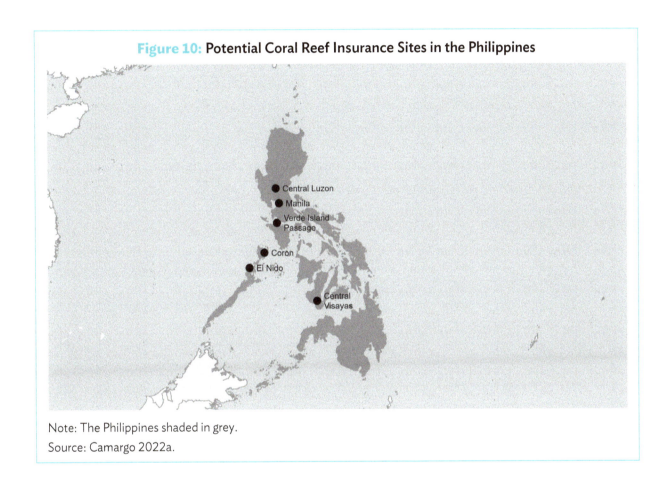

Figure 10: **Potential Coral Reef Insurance Sites in the Philippines**

Note: The Philippines shaded in grey.
Source: Camargo 2022a.

Across the Philippines, about 73,000 people are protected by reefs each year (Camargo 2022a). Coral reefs avert about $590 million in damages to build infrastructure annually (Beck et al. 2018). In addition, the tourism, recreation, and fisheries sector all benefit from coral reef ecosystems, and, beyond the market, fishing remains an important source of livelihood for many communities (Camargo 2022b, Roa-Quiaoit 2021).

Coral reefs in the Philippines are threatened by several insurable risks, including tropical cyclones, marine heatwaves and cold-water anomalies, tsunamis, volcanic eruption, and earthquakes (Camargo 2022a). In El Nido, a bleaching event in 1997–1998 caused a 16% decrease in live coral cover, resulting in an estimated revenue loss of $30,000 (Roa-Quiaoit 2021). And, in 2013, Super Typhoon Yolanda passed directly over Coron Island causing severe damage to the coral reefs and land-based infrastructure (Box 2) (Roa-Quiaoit 2021).

Stakeholders in the Philippines may be interested in repairing damaged reefs, given the recent efforts there to develop a sustainable financing scheme for mangroves that also includes an insurance component (Camargo 2022b). Purchasing insurance is not customary in the Philippines and, thus, the resilience insurance scheme is likely not well suited to the country (Camargo 2022b). However, the Philippine insurance market may be sufficiently well organized and regulated to facilitate the development of other innovative coral reef insurance schemes (Camargo 2022a). For example, the Philippine Catastrophe Insurance Facility was recently established to pool catastrophe risk and parametric catastrophe insurance has been issued under the Philippines Parametric Catastrophe Risk Insurance Programme (Camargo 2022b). Additionally, the appetite for innovative insurance products among local insurers is evidenced by their development of innovative products to cover agricultural damage from typhoons, the establishment of the Restoration Insurance Service Company to focus on green and gray infrastructure insurance, and the development of the Philippines Insurance Platform for Nature-based Resilience by the Earth Security Group and the Philippines Insurers and Reinsurers' Association.

Table 14 summarizes the key characteristics of these six sites in the Philippines related to their feasibility for the development of a coral reef insurance policy.

Table 14: Key Characteristics of Seven Potential Sites for an Insurance Policy in the Philippines

	Central Luzon	Central Visayas	Coron	El Nido	Manila	Verde Island Passage
1. Coral reefs provide a valuable service to people and the economy.						
Flood-protection value	Site-level assessments needed.					
Tourism and recreation ($ million annual revenue to local government)[a]			$165.60	$178.70		
2. The services provided by coral reefs are diminished by the occurrence of an insurable hazard.						
Earthquakes[b]	Yes	Yes			Yes	Yes
Marine heatwaves[c]			Yes	Yes		
Tropical cyclones[d]	Yes	Yes	Yes	Yes	Yes	Yes
Tsunamis[b]	Yes	Yes	Yes	Yes	Yes	
Volcanic eruptions[b]	Yes	Yes			Yes	Yes
3. The cost of repairing the reef damage is less than the losses in service provision.						
	Additional assessment required.					
4. The beneficiaries and/or parties responsible for managing the coral reefs are interested in restoring the damages.						
	Government agencies and some private sector actors in the Philippines have considered insurance within a broader disaster risk financing framework. However, unless justifiable rational is provided by coastal managers, the central government appears not to support active coral restoration practices and instead prefers to allow coral reefs to recover naturally (also known as passive restoration). The nongovernment organization Philippines Locally Managed Marine Area Network is dedicated to sustainable management of marine ecosystems.[e]					

continued on next page

Table 14: *Continued*

	Central Luzon	Central Visayas	Coron	El Nido	Manila	Verde Island Passage

5. The beneficiaries have the capacity to pay for an insurance premium.

    Additional assessment is required. In the absence of beneficiaries contributing directly to the purchase of the policy, there may be opportunities to raise funds via government funding mechanisms (e.g., environmental taxes, mitigation costs, ecosystem development fees) though this may require modifying legislation describing the purpose for which the collected funds can be used.[e]

6. The beneficiaries are entitled to buy a coral reef insurance policy.

    Additional assessment required. However, the Philippines has one of the lowest insurance penetration rates in all of Asia, so interest may be limited.[e]

[a] GEF 2021.
[b] Philippine Institute of Volcanology and Seismology. Earthquake- & Volcano-Related Maps. https://gisweb.phivolcs.dost.gov.ph/gisweb/earthquake-volcano-related-hazard-gis-information# (accessed 3 May 2023).
[c] Roa-Quiaoit 2021.
[d] Camargo 2022b and Roa-Quiaoit 2021.
[e] Camargo 2022b.
Source: Information in table compiled by The Nature Conservancy.

Solomon Islands

In Solomon Islands, 87% of the 600,000 people lead a subsistence lifestyle. Many of these people rely on fish and other marine resources for sustenance, livelihood, or income. Tourism, recreation, and fisheries also all benefit from coral reef ecosystems (Camargo 2022a). To date, at least one site in the country, the Arnavon Community Marine Park, has been identified as potentially suitable for a coral reef insurance pilot policy (Figure 11).

Coral reefs in Solomon Islands are threatened by several insurable risks, including tropical cyclones, marine heatwaves and cold-water anomalies, tsunamis, volcanic eruption, and earthquakes (Camargo 2022a). Tropical cyclones are frequent near Solomon Islands—with more than 100 since 1980. The country is within the Pacific Ring of Fire, so named due to its volcanoes and tectonic fault lines, and thus susceptible to seismic activity and tsunamis. In the past, earthquakes and tsunamis have reportedly uplifted reef flats, exposing them to the air and severely impacting fisheries-related activities.

Coastal communities seem increasingly aware that intact coastal ecosystems, such as coral reefs and mangroves, buffer coastlines from the impacts of extreme weather. This recognition has led to increasing support for community based natural resource management in the Solomon Islands. However, there is no national coral reef system data associated with socioeconomic values, no rigorous monitoring in place, and no restoration or post-cyclone reef repair. In particular, the Arnavon Community Marine Park has an existing management committee, and it may be possible to create a sub-account under the Arnavons Endowment Fund dedicated to coral reef financing and climate adaptation.

The 2010 Protected Areas Act also opened the possibility to establish trust funds, which could potentially purchase parametric insurance and manage payouts.

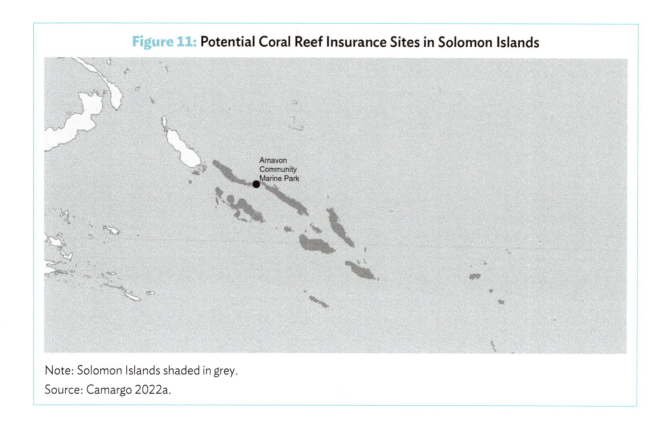

Figure 11: Potential Coral Reef Insurance Sites in Solomon Islands

Note: Solomon Islands shaded in grey.
Source: Camargo 2022a.

Table 15 summarizes the key characteristics of Arnavon Community Marine Park related to its feasibility for the development of a coral reef insurance policy.

Table 15: Key Characteristics of Potential Site for an Insurance Policy in Solomon Islands

Arnavon Community Marine Park (ACMP)	
1. Coral reefs provide a valuable service to people and the economy.	
Flood-protection value	Site-level assessments needed, but local data may be available.
Tourism and recreation	Providing equitable and sustainable livelihood benefits to the surrounding communities, employing conservation rangers and is a tourism and education/research destination. A local woman's group, KAWAKI, manages a project to expand the ecotourism operation.
2. The services provided by coral reefs are diminished by the occurrence of an insurable hazard.	
Earthquakes	Yes
Marine heatwaves	Yes
Tropical cyclones	Yes
Tsunamis	Yes
Volcanic eruptions	Yes

continued on next page

Table 15: *Continued*

Arnavon Community Marine Park (ACMP)
3. The cost of repairing the reef damage is less than the losses in service provision.
Additional assessment required.
4. The beneficiaries and/or parties responsible for managing the coral reefs are interested in restoring the damages.
The reef is wholly owned by Solomon Islands government and was officially designated a protected area in the Protected Areas Act of 2010. More broadly in Solomon Islands, engagement with local clan or tribe members would be required since the customary tenure system permits local clans and tribes to own and manage patches of reefs.
5. The beneficiaries have the capacity to pay for an insurance premium.
The operations at ACMP are financed by the Arnavons Endowment Fund; however, the annual dividend payments are insufficient to cover the full annual costs of operation. The yearly shortfall has been covered by philanthropic efforts, though this represents a significant risk to the long-term operation of ACMP. A thorough evaluation of innovative financial schemes is needed to identify sustainable means of contributing to the endowment fund and/or supporting ongoing conservation efforts.
6. The beneficiaries are entitled to buy a coral reef insurance policy.
Additional assessment is required to determine who, or which entities may be entitled to purchase a coral reef insurance policy. Parametric insurance has been deployed at the national level in the Solomon Islands, although the initiative through which it was implemented, the Pacific Catastrophe Risk Assessment and Financing Initiative, has since discontinued. Insurance companies in the Solomon Islands, like elsewhere, tend only to cover infrastructure and losses, and do so mainly in the capital city and other provincial centers.

Source: Camargo 2022a.

Fiji

The coral reefs in Fiji not only provide critical protective value but also provide significant benefits to the tourism, recreation, and fisheries sectors (Camargo 2022a). Fiji was identified as a top-tier candidate country to explore potential to develop an insurance scheme as part of an overarching risk management and sustainable funding strategy for protection and conservation of coral reefs within existing marine protected areas and marine and coastal heritage sites (Camargo 2022a). To date, four potential sites have been identified for such a reef insurance policy (Figure 12).

Fiji's reefs systems are threatened by cyclones and coral bleaching events and, Fiji's tourism, recreation, and fisheries sectors would likely be impacted by such disaster events (ADB 2020b, Camargo 2022a). In 2016, Tropical Cyclone Winston made landfall on the main island of Viti Levu, with wind speeds of 233 kilometers per hour. The storm significantly damaged coral reefs near Northern Lau, resulting in "rubble fields" of coral that continued to move with the tides and cause additional damage and significant damage up to 20–30 meters below the surface (ADB 2020b).

Figure 12: Potential Coral Reef Insurance Sites in Fiji

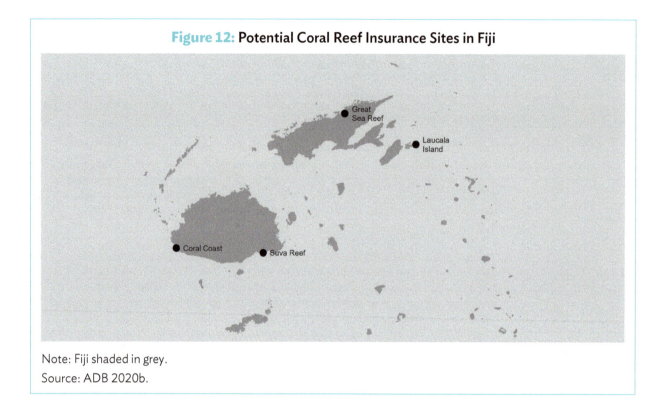

Note: Fiji shaded in grey.
Source: ADB 2020b.

Table 16 summarizes the key characteristics of these four sites in Fiji related to their feasibility for the development of a coral reef insurance policy.

Table 16: Key Characteristics of Potential Sites for an Insurance Policy in Fiji

	Coral Coast	Great Sea Reef	Laucala Island	Suva Reef
1. Coral reefs provide a valuable service to people and the economy.				
Flood-protection value	Site-level assessments needed. Previous estimates have shown that over half of Fiji's population directly benefits from protection by coral reefs.[a]			
Tourism and recreation	Marine tourism is estimated to provide $574 million annually and support about 41,500 jobs. Coral reef and lagoon tourism alone was valued at about $407 million, over 70% of all marine tourism.[b] The Great Sea Reef is home to about 70% of Fiji's tourism.[c]			
Fishing	Subsistence food provision from inshore fisheries, small scale inshore commercial fisheries, and commercial offshore fisheries generate about $30 million, $27 million, and $10 million annually, respectively.[b] The Great Sea Reef contributes about 80% of Fiji's offshore fishing revenue and coastal inhabitants as well as the broader Fiji population rely on the inshore fisheries for nutrition and livelihoods.[b]			
2. The services provided by coral reefs are diminished by the occurrence of an insurable hazard.				
Earthquakes				
Marine heatwaves	Yes	Yes	Yes	Yes
Tropical cyclones	Yes	Yes	Yes	Yes
Tsunamis				
Volcanic eruptions				

continued on next page

Table 16: *Continued*

	Coral Coast	Great Sea Reef	Laucala Island	Suva Reef

3. The cost of repairing the reef damage is less than the losses in service provision.

    Additional assessment required.

4. The beneficiaries and/or parties responsible for managing the coral reefs are interested in restoring the damages.

    Several resorts and tourism operators in Fiji are actively preserving and protecting marine environments, such as Nukukbati, Kaibu, Laucala Island Resorts, and the Vatuvara Foundation. The Fiji Locally Managed Marine Areas, a national network of organizations and traditional indigenous iTaukei promoting preservation and protection, also helped to establishment a blue economic zone plan, which may include an insurance component near Suva reef.[d] Additionally, government agencies and some private sector actors have considered insurance within broader disaster risk financing framework.[b]

5. The beneficiaries have the capacity to pay for an insurance premium.

    Additional assessment required although initial discussions are positive.[b] Additionally, engagements are ongoing within Fiji about climate change adaptation, disaster risk reduction, and disaster risk financing, in which insurance is considered a potential option.[e]

6. The beneficiaries are entitled to buy a coral reef insurance policy.

    Additional assessment required. However, a special purpose vehicle may be permitted to purchase a policy on behalf of a group of beneficiaries; Fiji's laws and regulations provide several options for establishing a special purpose vehicle.[f] In addition, Fiji's insurance market appears sufficiently well organized and regulated to facilitate the deployment of coral reef insurance product. Fiji's insurance regulator, the Reserve Bank of Fiji, oversees all insurance regulations, and approves parametric insurance for Fiji's private sector; the Reserve Bank of Fiji has approved at least one parametric product with an offshore provider that utilizes wind speeds to trigger payouts.[b]

[a] Spalding, Brumbaugh, and Landis 2016.
[b] ADB 2020b.
[c] Young and Wharton 2020.
[d] GEF 2021.
[e] Camargo 2022a.
[f] ADB 2020b and GEF 2021.

Source: Information in table compiled by The Nature Conservancy.

B. Broader Opportunities across Asia and the Pacific

Beyond Indonesia, the Philippines, Solomon Islands, and Fiji, coral reefs provide valuable flood protection benefits to local communities in many countries in Asia and the Pacific (Figure 13). Some of these with the highest numbers of people protected from coral reefs include Malaysia, the People's Republic of China, Thailand, Viet Nam, and many of the Pacific's small island developing states, such as Palau, Samoa, Tonga, and Vanuatu. In many of these countries, coral reefs are a crucial component of the economy and livelihoods through a strong tourism industry and/or through strong dependence on fisheries (Figure 14). In the remainder of this subsection, we focus on coral reefs in Malaysia, the People's Republic of China, Thailand, Viet Nam, Palau, Samoa, Tonga, and Vanuatu. While not exhaustive, these countries represent a starting point for exploring coral reef insurance more broadly in Asia and the Pacific.

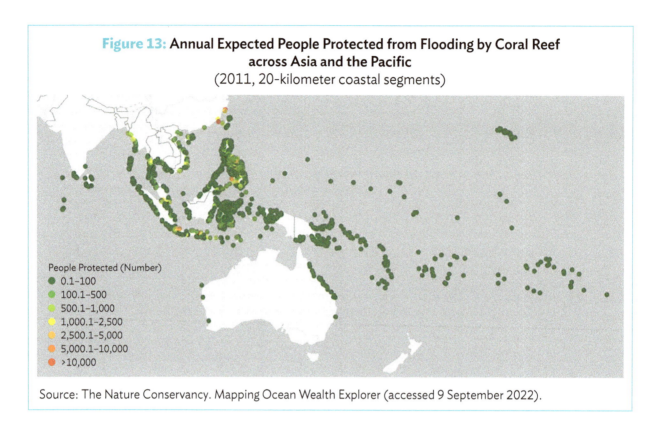

Figure 13: Annual Expected People Protected from Flooding by Coral Reef across Asia and the Pacific
(2011, 20-kilometer coastal segments)

Source: The Nature Conservancy. Mapping Ocean Wealth Explorer (accessed 9 September 2022).

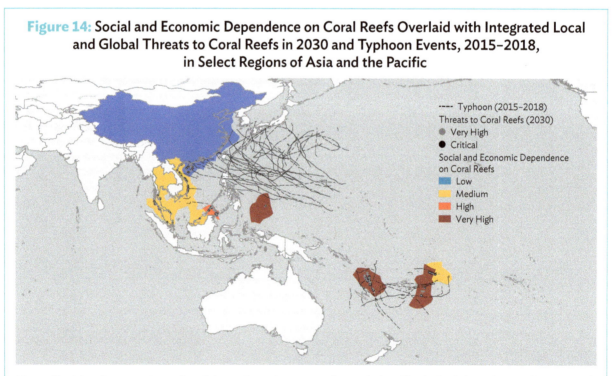

Figure 14: Social and Economic Dependence on Coral Reefs Overlaid with Integrated Local and Global Threats to Coral Reefs in 2030 and Typhoon Events, 2015–2018, in Select Regions of Asia and the Pacific

Notes: Social and economic coral reef dependence is measured as an index. The index is based on reef-associated population, reef fisheries employment, reef-associated exports, nutritional dependence on fish and seafood, reef-associated tourism, and shoreline protection. Integrated local and global threats to coral reefs include local threats from coastal development, marine-based pollution and damage, watershed-based pollution, overfishing and destructive fishing, thermal stress, and acidification. A typhoon refers to storms with maximum wind speeds in excess of 118 kilometers per hour.

Sources: Burke et al. 2011b; Burke 2011a; created by The Nature Conservancy from corresponding "Global Threats" GIS data set; and ReliefWeb 2019.

As noted, many of the coral reefs in these regions are highly exposed. Figure 14 overlays the social and economic dependence in these regions with a map of coral reefs that will be very highly or critically threatened by 2030 and with the storm tracks of typhoons that occurred in these areas between 2015 and 2018. All of the regions contain coral reefs that are highly or critically threatened and many of the regions are highly exposed to typhoons—most notably the People's Republic of China, Samoa, Tonga, and Vanuatu. Given this evidence, it is highly likely that there are locations within each of these regions where the first essential criteria for ensuring reefs—showing that the coral reef needs insurance—would be met. A local-level analysis would be needed to determine if the cost of repairing any given coral reef was less than the benefits.

The second essential criteria—are there potential buyers of the coral reef insurance policy—is more difficult to determine in the absence of a localized analysis. A preliminary assessment by Camargo (2022a, pp. 49–50), however, showed that:

- The People's Republic of China, Thailand, and Viet Nam all have strong involvement from the community in the conservation of marine coastal ecosystems.
- A disaster risk financing framework exists in Viet Nam, where insurance could be seen as a critical component.
- Tonga, Vanuatu, and Viet Nam are all actively engaged at the international, regional, and national level to protect marine coastal ecosystems.
- The insurance markets in the People's Republic of China and Viet Nam are becoming more robust.

In many of these countries, however, how to best fund any premium costs of an insurance policy remains a critical issue. Many countries, and communities within these countries, are not likely to have sufficient resources to pay into insurance on their own so a robust revenue source will be needed to ensure premium payments can be made. While these observations are not proof of the viability of an insurance policy in any of these regions, they indicate potential for an insurance policy.

VIII

EXPANDING TO OTHER COASTAL ECOSYSTEMS

Likely not the only coastal ecosystem where innovative funding sources, such as insurance, could be developed. Other critical coastal ecosystems provide valuable services to coastal communities and assets.

A. Mangroves

Globally, there are nearly 14 million hectares of mangrove forests across 118 countries (Spalding 2010). Mangrove forests are generally located in the inter-tidal region between sea and land in tropical and subtropical regions of the globe between 30°N and 30°S (Giri et al. 2010). Today, mangroves are at increasing risk from direct and indirect human activities. The primary driver of mangrove loss worldwide is mangrove clearing for aquaculture or urban settlements; almost 80% of this mangrove clearing occurs in just the following countries, all of which are in Asia and the Pacific: Indonesia, Malaysia, the Philippines, Thailand, and Viet Nam (Goldberg et al. 2020). Outside of these six countries, the primary drivers of mangrove loss are erosion and tropical storms (Goldberg et al. 2020). In addition, mangrove habitats are threatened by impacts from climate change, including temperature increases, precipitation changes, and sea-level rise (Ward et al. 2016, Saintilan et al. 2020).

During tropical storms, mangrove forests serve as the first line of coastal defense. Their root systems can help stabilize soils and reduce erosion and mangrove forests dissipate wave energy and slow storm surge penetration. The first 100 meters of a mangrove forest can reduce wave height up to 66% (McIvor et al. 2012). Globally, mangroves have been shown to provide over $65 billion in flood protection benefits annually and to protect over 15 million people (Menéndez et al. 2020). In a more detailed analysis of the Philippines, scientists estimated that mangroves provide over $1 billion in flood protection benefits annually and protect over half a million people (Menéndez et al. 2018).

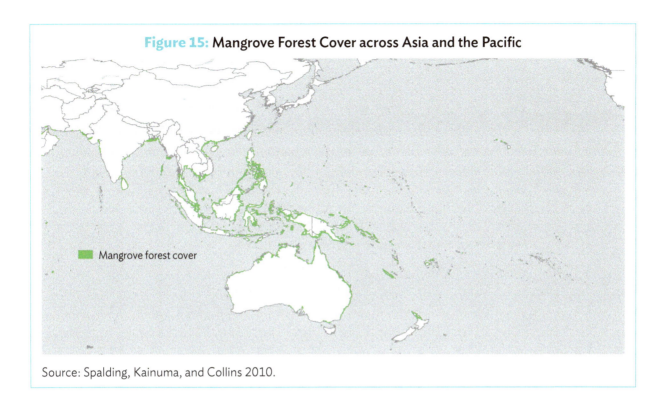

Figure 15: Mangrove Forest Cover across Asia and the Pacific

Source: Spalding, Kainuma, and Collins 2010.

In addition, mangrove forests serve as important nurseries for many reef fish populations and store a disproportionate amount of carbon relative to their land cover (Hutchison et al. 2014). Over 40% of global mangroves are estimated to be in Asia and the Pacific, making the region a key area to explore the applicability of an insurance product (Figure 15) (Giri et al. 2010). Initial feasibility assessments in the Gulf of Mexico and Caribbean have demonstrated the potential for a mangrove insurance policy there (Box 8).

Box 8

Feasibility of Mangrove Insurance in Gulf of Mexico and Caribbean

The Nature Conservancy, in collaboration with AXA XL and University of California Santa Cruz, undertook a prefeasibility and feasibility assessment to better understand the potential for a mangrove insurance policy in the Gulf of Mexico and Caribbean. The prefeasibility assessment identified Mexico, Florida, and The Bahamas as the three locations with some of the largest areas of mangroves that would be cost-effective to restore and with favorable local market and governance conditions.[a]

In the feasibility study, the team identified more than 1,200 kilometers of coastline where mangroves would be cost-effective to restore, including 500 kilometers of coastline, spanning over 500,000 hectares of mangroves, in Mexico; 600 kilometers of coastline, spanning nearly 20,000 hectares of mangroves, in Florida; and 60 kilometers of coastline, spanning nearly 3,000 hectares of mangroves in The Bahamas.[b]

continued on next page

Box 8 *continued*

This spatial analysis was accompanied by stakeholder engagements in each of the three regions. Through these stakeholder conversations, the team identified nine sites as potential sites for a mangrove insurance pilot policy—based on the presence of large areas of mangroves, the high protection value of mangroves, and strong interest from local stakeholders.

Subsequent phases of the work will focus on the design of a mangrove insurance policy at one or more of these potential sites. In the design phase, the team will consider how best to structure a mangrove insurance policy. In particular, one needs to determine whether a parametric or indemnity policy is more appropriate for mangrove insurance. Recent research suggests that inland coastal areas susceptible to hydrologic isolation could experience mangrove dieback 6 months following a storm event, suggesting that a combined parametric-indemnity policy may be most appropriate.[c]

[a] Beck et al. 2020.
[b] Rogers et al. 2022.
[c] Lagomasino et al. 2021.

B. Salt Marshes

Globally, there are over 5 million hectares of salt marshes across 99 countries (Mcowen et al. 2017). Salt marshes consist predominately of salt-tolerant grasses, herbs, and low shrubs. They are intertidal coastal ecosystems, primarily in middle and high latitudes, that are frequently flooded with salt or brackish waters. Globally, nearly 50% of salt marshes have been degraded or lost (Barbier et al. 2011, 180). Historically, many salt marshes were filled for urban or agricultural development. Today, coastal development, dredging, and pollution all threaten salt marsh ecosystems; sea-level rise poses the biggest climate-related threat to salt marshes (Kirwan and Megonigal 2013; Weis, Segarra, and Bernal 2016).

Like mangroves, salt marshes can serve as a natural barrier to tropical storms. They can attenuate wave energy, slow and store floodwaters, and prevent erosion (Gedan et al. 2011, Weis et al. 2016). In addition, salt marshes remove sediment, nutrients, and other contaminants from runoff and riverine discharge, effectively serving as a natural water filter. In many areas of the world, they provide important habitat for livestock grazing and provide important habitat for fisheries. In particular, salt marshes host young fish, crab, shrimp, and shellfish because the dense plant structures make salt marshes inaccessible to many large fish (Barbier et al. 2011, Weis et al. 2016). Finally, salt marshes are one of the most productive ecosystems in the world and sequester millions of tons of carbon annually (Barbier et al. 2011). In much of the tropics and subtropics, including areas in Asia and the Pacific, salt marshes are replaced by mangroves (Figure 16). Particularly in the People's Republic of China, however, there are large areas of salt marshes—over 127,000 hectares—likely providing significant benefits to nearby populations (Hu et al. 2021).

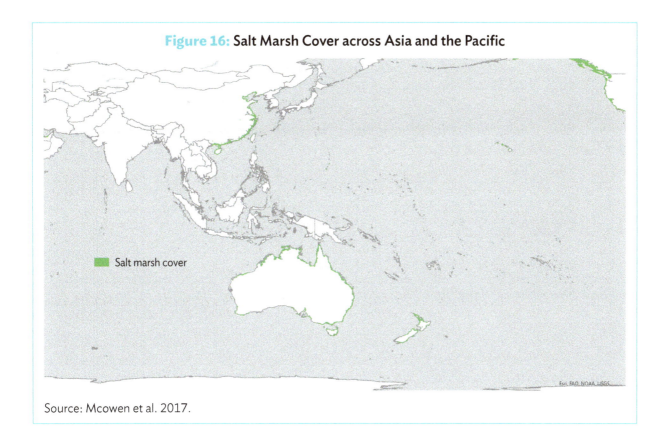

Figure 16: Salt Marsh Cover across Asia and the Pacific

Source: Mcowen et al. 2017.

C. Oysters

Oysters are bi-valve mollusks that live in marine or brackish waters. They are known as a keystone species because their presence is critical to the survival of many other marine species. In aggregation, oysters make up oyster reefs, which are composed of living and dead oyster shells. Oyster reefs are distributed globally in intertidal and shallow subtidal zones in both estuaries and along coastlines across tropical and temperate environments (Gillies et al. 2020). A review of over 144 bays and 55 ecoregions globally found that 85% of oyster reefs have been lost (Beck et al. 2011). Oysters have been lost due to overharvesting, reef degradation during harvest, and changes in hydrology and water conditions from shoreline modification and pollution (Gillies et al. 2020).

Oyster reefs are three-dimensional structures that essentially function as living breakwaters and are the ecological equivalent of coral reefs in higher latitudes and estuarine environments in the tropics (Grabowski et al. 2012, Chan et al. 2022, Lowe et al. 2021). Oysters have also been shown to grow faster than sea-level rise, effectively making them a natural defense against shoreline erosion (Rodriguez et al. 2014). Oyster reefs also provide immense water quality services through their ability to remove nitrogen, remove phytoplankton, and enhance seagrass (Grabowski et al. 2012). And, in addition to being a direct source of food through oyster harvesting, oyster reefs are important habitat for many fish and crustaceans. Ten square meters of restored oyster reefs can provide over additional 2 kilograms of fish and crustacean production annually (Peterson, Grabowski, and Powers 2003).

The economic value of services provided by oyster reefs, in a more general study that excluded harvesting, has been estimated at $5,500 to $99,000 per year with shoreline stabilization being the most valuable service provided by oyster reefs (Grabowski et al. 2012). More recently, a large-scale oyster reef restoration project in the Chesapeake Bay was found to have a return on investment of nearly 50% per year (Knoche et al. 2020). In Asia and the Pacific, oyster reefs can be found throughout southern and eastern Australia, New Zealand, along the Yellow Sea to Hong Kong, China and the Pearl River delta (Beck et al. 2011).

D. Sand Dunes

Coastal sand dunes are present along low-lying coasts and serve as a transition between terrestrial and marine environments. They form when ocean waves and wind transport sand to coasts that, when combined with vegetation, form coastal dunes. They typically are associated with sandy beaches, although the distribution of dune versus beach will differ across locations and are found in nearly all latitudes and cover roughly 34% of ice-free coastlines (Barbier et al. 2011). Globally, many coastal dune systems are severely degraded or have been lost completely (Martínez, Psuty, and Lubke 2008). Coastal dunes have largely been degraded and lost due to human pressure from demographic expansion and industrial growth—over 600 million people live in low-lying coastal zones globally (Martínez, Psuty, and Lubke 2008; United Nations 2022).

Coastal protection is the most valuable service provided by coastal dunes. As waves hit the coast, the beach slope attenuates waves and, at high tide, they are attenuated by the foredune. In addition, sand dunes stabilize sediment and soil retention, which limits coastal erosion. Sand dunes also provide raw materials; sand; support habitat for fish, shellfish, and birds; and provide water catchment and purification (Barbier et al. 2011). Finally, sand dunes and beaches are an important tourist attraction and source of recreational activities—80% of all tourism globally takes place in coastal areas (United Nations 2022). In Asia and the Pacific, much of the regions coastal dune systems are in Australia, New Zealand, and southern People's Republic of China (Martínez et al. 2021). Very few dunes exist in Thailand and Malaysia and there is only one area of significant dune development in the Philippines (Hesp 2008). The main reasons for lack of coastal dunes in these regions is believed to be a combination of weak offshore winds, lack of any real dry season, and limited supply of sand.

IX

CONCLUSION

In 2019, ADB launched the Healthy Oceans and Sustainable Blue Economy Action plan with a commitment of scaling up its investments and technical assistance in this area to $5 billion by 2024.

Coastal and Marine Ecosystem Resilience, as one of the flagship programs under the action plan, recognizes that urgent action is needed in response to the dual crises of rapid biodiversity loss and climate change. Massive investment at scale is needed in both nature and transformational adaptation to build the resilience of Asia and the Pacific's critical coastal and marine ecosystems, communities, cities, and island nations to climate- and disaster-related shocks and stresses. Nature-based solutions—such as the protection and restoration of coral reefs, mangrove forests, wetlands, and sandy beaches—enhance ecosystem resilience and the protection of coastal cities and communities while providing multiple economic, societal, and climate mitigation co-benefits (ADB 2022b).

Ocean finance is critical for minimizing the funding gap to achieve healthy and resilient oceans in the region and to strengthen the enabling environment for blue economies. Subregional sector-specific initiatives include ADB's Finance Sector Group's support for small and medium-sized enterprises (SMEs) to make ocean investments. SMEs dominate the ocean economy, as in the main economy, comprising up to 90% of enterprises and 70% of employment, yet SMEs suffer from too little access to capital and technical support. Therefore, the Finance Sector Group has developed an SME-blended finance platform—SME BlueImpact Asia—to complement the core business of financing large public projects. This initiative requires unique skill sets to build SME pipelines across blue sectors and ADB regions, using accelerators, digital technologies, and matching private capital. Several blue private sector SME projects have already been identified among others in the area of Coastal and Marine Ecosystem Resilience with deeper community involvement thanks to SME engagement in marine protected areas that includes coral reefs.

Comprehensive reef management will include financing of reef management, reef restoration, and post-disaster reef repair in addition to policy work aimed at improving legislation to address the reduction and management of impacts to reefs, such as reductions in nutrient loads or wastewater pollution.

While, in the long term, changes in policy to better address the root cause of coral reef damage will be critical to their conservation and restoration, this report focuses on innovative means of financing reef management, restoration, and repair.

The financing of reef management, for example, should not be detrimental to the financing of reef restoration and post-disaster reef repair. In general, reef management and reef restoration are financed before post-disaster reef repair. However, until a full risk management financing system is in place, effective progress will not be made in reef management and reef restoration as a single disaster event can wipe out years, or decades, of progress in the first two components. Funding the full suite of a reef's management, restoration, and repair needs will require a holistic approach and the use of a number of different funding sources.

An overarching reef risk management strategy will help reef managers and beneficiaries of the reef's ecosystem services assess the risks faced by particular coral reefs and determine the most cost-effective funding sources to manage these risks. The following steps can be followed to develop a coral reef risk management strategy:

(i)   Assess and understand the risks to the identified coral reefs.
(ii) Determine the extent and probability of physical damage and/or economic impact that each risk may cause.
(iii) Identify the needed response to reduce damage to coral reefs and to the economy.
(iv) Assess the cost of these response efforts. Compare these costs to the estimated losses that would occur without the reef in place.
(v)   Compare the costs and benefits of financial schemes and select those providing the highest rate of return. Several innovative funding sources may be chosen. For example, insurance policies could be paired with emergency funds and other local resources to effectively fund reef management, restoration, and post-disaster repair (Figure 17).

Insurance is increasingly seen as an opportunity to integrate private capital into the protection and maintenance of ecosystems and the services or benefits they provide to people. For coral reefs, insurance payouts following a disaster event from a natural hazard can be used to quickly fund the restoration and repair of damaged reefs. With rapid response post-damage restoration, coral reefs are able to more quickly recover from damage. In some instances, coral reefs may be unable to recover naturally without active restoration. In this report, we have highlighted both the need for innovative funding courses, such as insurance, to fund post-disaster reef repair, and the potential opportunities for such schemes in Asia and the Pacific.

Based on the analyses highlighted in this report, insurance is likely to emerge as a cost-effective financial risk management instrument for many coral reefs in Asia and the Pacific, particularly in Indonesia, the Philippines, Solomon Islands, and Fiji. Following the adoption of parametric insurance coverage in Quintana Roo, Mexico, insurance has proven able to provide immediate funds to effectively respond to damage events from natural hazards impacting coral reefs. However, developing a specific coral reef insurance policy can take time and requires many steps (Figure 18).

CONCLUSION 59

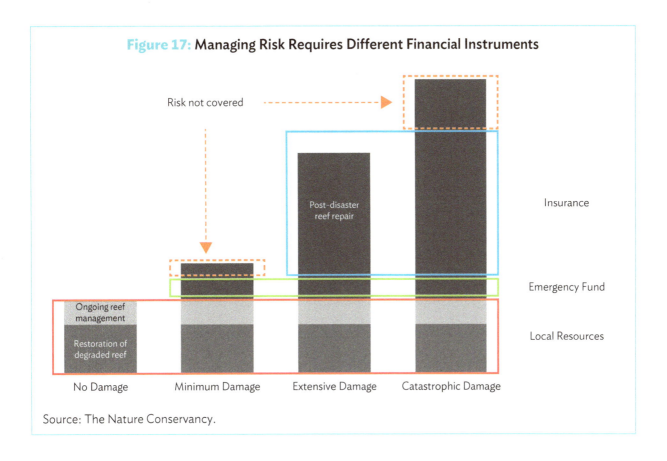

Figure 17: Managing Risk Requires Different Financial Instruments

Source: The Nature Conservancy.

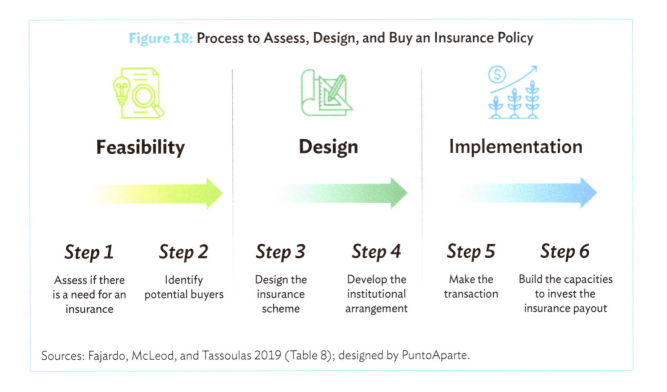

Figure 18: Process to Assess, Design, and Buy an Insurance Policy

Feasibility → **Design** → **Implementation**

Step 1 — Assess if there is a need for an insurance

Step 2 — Identify potential buyers

Step 3 — Design the insurance scheme

Step 4 — Develop the institutional arrangement

Step 5 — Make the transaction

Step 6 — Build the capacities to invest the insurance payout

Sources: Fajardo, McLeod, and Tassoulas 2019 (Table 8); designed by PuntoAparte.

In addition, comparable parametric insurance policies developed in the past—such as those in Mexico, Mesoamerican Reef, and Hawaii—have focused on justifying the cost-effectiveness of the insurance policy based on the value of the physical assets protected. To more rapidly scale nature-based insurance globally, we must better understand how these existing models contribute to community resilience and protection of the most climate-vulnerable populations. Future iterations of nature-based insurance will then be better able to provide tangible benefits to the most climate-vulnerable populations with a focus on diversity, equity, inclusion, and climate justice. The work in this report provides initial insights into the feasibility phase of this development process.

Work in Asia and the Pacific will need to focus on more detailed site-specific assessments of the feasibility of coral reef insurance, the design of such a policy, and the local capacity and institutional arrangements needed to manage the purchase of such a policy.

REFERENCES

Alvarez-Filip, L., N. A. Estrada-Saldívar, E. Pérez-Cervantes, F. Javier González-Barrios, and F. S. Fajardo. 2021. *Comparative Analysis of Risks Faced by the World's Coral Reefs.* UNAM-The Nature Conservancy.

Andersson, A. J. and D. Gledhill. 2013. Ocean Acidification and Coral Reefs: Effects on Breakdown, Dissolution, and Net Ecosystem Calcification. *Annual Review of Marine Science.* 5: pp. 321–348. https://doi.org/10.1146/annurev-marine-121211-172241.

Anticamara, J. A. and K. T. B. Go. 2017. Impacts of Super-Typhoon Yolanda on Philippine Reefs and Communities. *Regional Environmental Change.* 17(3): pp. 703–713. https://doi.org/10.1007/s10113-016-1062-8.

Asian Development Bank (ADB). 2019. ADB Introduces Contingent Disaster Financing for Natural Disasters. Press release. 1 August. https://www.adb.org/news/adb-introduces-contingent-disaster-financing-natural-disasters#:~:text=CDF%E2%80%94approved%20today%20by%20ADB%E2%80%99s%20Board%20of%20Directors%E2%80%94will%20cover,to%20be%20completed%20before%20a%20natural%20disaster%20occurs.

———. 2020a. *Financing Disaster Risk Reduction in Asia and the Pacific, A Guide for Policy Makers.* Manila. https://www.adb.org/sites/default/files/institutional-document/670596/financing-disaster-risk-reduction-asia-pacific.pdf.

———. 2020b. *Strengthening Climate and Disaster Resilience of Investments in the Pacific—Public–Private Partnerships for Coral Reef Insurance in Fiji.* Manila.

———. 2022a. *Financing the Blue Economy, Investments in Sustainable Blue Small-Medium Enterprises and Projects in Asia and the Pacific.* Manila. https://dx.doi.org/10.22617/TCS220281-2.

———. 2022b. *Healthy Oceans Implementation Plan 2022–2024.* Manila. https://www.adb.org/sites/default/files/institutional-document/850721/healthy-oceans-implementation-plan-2022-2024.pdf.

Asner, G. P., N. R. Vaughn, J. Heckler, D. E. Knapp, C. Balzotti, E. Shafron, R. E. Martin, B. J. Neilson, and J. M. Gove. 2020. Large-Scale Mapping of Live Corals to Guide Reef Conservation. *PNAS.* 117(52): pp. 33711–33718. https://doi.org/10.1073/pnas.2017628117.

Barbier, E., S. D. Hacker, C. Kennedy, E. W. Koch, A. C. Stier, and B. R. Sillman. 2011. The Value of Estuarine and Coastal Ecosystem Services. *Ecological Monographs.* 81(2): pp. 169–193. https://doi.org/10.1890/10-1510.1.

Beck, M. W., R. D. Brumbaugh, L. Airoldi, A. Carranza, L. D. Coen, C. Crawford, O. Defeo, G. J. Edgar, B. Hancock, and M. C. Kayal. 2011. Oyster Reefs at Risk and Recommendations for Conservation, Restoration, and Management. *Bioscience.* 61(2): pp. 107–116. https://doi.org/10.1525/bio.2011.61.2.5.

REFERENCES

Beck, M. W., N. Heck, S. Narayan, P. Menéndez, S. Torres-Ortega, I. J. Losada, M. Way, M. Rogers, and L. McFarlane-Connelly. 2020. *Reducing Caribbean Risk: Opportunities for Cost-Effective Mangrove Restoration and Insurance*. Arlington VA: The Nature Conservancy. https://www.nature.org/content/dam/tnc/nature/en/documents/TNC_MangroveInsurance_Final.pdf.

Beck, M. W., I. J. Losada, P. Menéndez, B. G. Reguero, P. Díaz-Simal, and F. Fernández. 2018. The Global Flood Protection Savings Provided by Coral Reefs. *Nature Communications*. 9: p. 2186. https://doi.org/10.1038/s41467-018-04568-z.

Bergh, C., L. Bertolotti, T. Bieri, J. Bowman, R. Braun, J. Cardillo, M. Chaudhury, K. Falinksi, L. Geselbracht, and K. Hum. 2020. *Insurance for Natural Infrastructure: Assessing the Feasibility of Insuring Coral Reefs in Florida and Hawai'i*. Arlington, VA: The Nature Conservancy. https://www.nature.org/content/dam/tnc/nature/en/documents/TNC_BOA_ReefInsuranceFeasibility_FLHI_113020.pdf.

Blundell, A. 2010. Reef Ball Type Cemetery Allows for Burial at Sea for your Cremated Remains. 15 April. https://reefbuilders.com/2010/04/15/reef-ball-cemetery-burial-at-sea/.

Boström-Einarsson, L., R. C. Babcock, E. Bayraktarov, D. Ceccarelli, N. Cook, S. CA Ferse, and B. Hancock. 2020. Coral Restoration—A Systematic Review of Current Methods, Successes, Failures and Future Directions. *PloS One*. 15(1): p. e0226631. https://doi.org/10.1371/journal.pone.0226631.

Burke, L., K. Reytar, M. Spalding, and A. Perry. 2011a. *Reefs At Risk Revisited*. Washington, DC: World Resources Institute. https://files.wri.org/d8/s3fs-public/pdf/reefs_at_risk_revisited.pdf.

———. 2011b. *Reefs at Risk Revisited: Social and Economic Dependence on Coral Reefs*. World Resources Institute (accessed through Resource Watch on 10 September 2022). https://bit.ly/3snvK5o.

———. 2012. *Reefs At Risk Revisited in the Coral Triangle*. Washington, DC: World Resources Institute. https://files.wri.org/d8/s3fs-public/pdf/reefs_at_risk_revisited_coral_triangle.pdf.

Byrnes, T. A. and R. J. K. Dunn. 2020. Boating-and Shipping-Related Environmental Impacts and Example Management Measures: A Review. *Journal of Marine Science and Engineering*. 8(11): pp. 1–49. https://doi.org/10.3390/jmse8110908.

Camargo, A. 2022a. *Risk Transfer Solutions to Protect MCE and NBS Supporting Coastal Resilience*. Manila: Asian Development Bank.

———. 2022b. *Detailed Proposal, Risk Transfer Solutions to Protect Marine Coastal Ecosystems in the Philippines*. Manila: Asian Development Bank.

Chan, S. S. W., H. T. Wong, M. Thomas, H. K. Alleway, B. Hancock, and B. D. Russell. 2022. Increased Biodiversity Associated with Abandoned Benthic Oyster Farms Highlight Ecosystem Benefits of Both Oyster Reefs and Traditional Aquaculture. *The Ecological Function of Mariculture*. https://doi.org/10.3389/fmars.2022.862548.

Chapman, M. G. and A. J. Underwood. 2011. Evaluation of Ecological Engineering of "Armoured" Shorelines to Improve their Value as Habitat. *Journal of Experimental Marine Biology and Ecology*. 400(1–2): 302–313. https://doi.org/10.1016/j.jembe.2011.02.025.

Chavanich, S., E. Gomez, C. L. Ming, B. Goh, L. Tong Tan, K. Tun, T. Tai Chong, P. Cabaitan, J. Guest, and L. Ng. 2014. *Coral Restoration Techniques in the Western Pacific Region*. United Nations Educational, Scientific and Cultural Organization-IOC/WESTPAC, Bangkok. https://www.icriforum.org/wp-content/uploads/2020/11/coral-restoration-2014-PDF-low.pdf.

Chiu-Freund, S. 2009. El Nido's Miniloc Island Resort. *World Wildlife Fund*. 24 May. http://coraltriangle.blogs.panda.org/coral-reefs/el-nidos-miniloc-island-resort.

Climate Bonds Initiative. 2019. *Climate Resilience Principles, A Framework for Assessing Climate Resilience Investments*. Climate Bonds Initiative, World Resources Institute, Climate Resilience Consulting. https://www.climatebonds.net/files/page/files/climate-resilience-principles-climate-bonds-initiative-20190917-.pdf.

dela Cruz, D. W. and P. L. Harrison. 2017. Enhanced Larval Supply and Recruitment Can Replenish Reef Corals on Degraded Reefs. *Scientific Reports*. 7(1): pp. 1–13. https://doi.org/10.1038/s41598-017-14546-y.

Deutz, A., J. Kellet, and T. Zoltani. 2018. *Innovative Finance for Resilient Coasts and Communities*. The Nature Conservancy and United Nations Development Programme for Environment. https://www.nature.org/content/dam/tnc/nature/en/documents/Innovative_Finance_Resilient_Coasts_and_Communities.pdf.

Devlin-Durante, M. K., M. W. Miller, Caribbean Acropora Research Group, W. F. Precht, I. B. Baums, L. Carne, and T. B. Smith. 2016. How Old are You? Genet Age Estimates in a Clonal Animal. *Molecular Ecology*. 25(22): pp. 5628–5646. https://doi.org/10.1111/mec.13865.

Douglas, S. L., C. Ferraro, C. R. Dixon, L. Oliver, and L. Pitts. 2012. A Gulf of Mexico Marsh Restoration and Protection Project. In *33rd International Conference on Coastal Engineering*. https://doi.org/10.9753/icce.v33.management.76.

Edwards, A. and E. Gomez. 2007. *Reef Restoration Concepts and Guidelines: Making Sensible Management Choices in the Face of Uncertainty*. St. Lucia, Australia: The Coral Reef Targeted Research & Capacity Building for Management Program. https://eprints.ncl.ac.uk/file_store/production/1068/9E2CFF45-5912-481C-B974-A20454B506D5.pdf.

Epstein, N., R. P. M. Bak, and B. Rinkevich. 2001. Strategies for Gardening Denuded Coral Reef Areas: The Applicability of using Different Types of Coral Material for Reef Restoration. *Restoration Ecology*. 9(4): pp. 432–442. https://doi.org/10.1046/j.1526-100X.2001.94012.x.

Evans, S. 2021. Red Cross Targets Cat Bonds for Nature-Based Humanitarian Resilience Financing. *ARTEMIS*. 28 July. https://www.artemis.bm/news/red-cross-targets-cat-bonds-for-nature-based-humanitarian-resilience-financing/.

Fabian, R., M. Beck, and D. Potts. 2013. *Reef Restoration for Coastal Defense: A Review*. Santa Cruz: University of California, Santa Cruz. http://car-spaw-rac.org/IMG/pdf/Reef_restoration_Coastal_Defense_report_Final-2.pdf.

Fajardo, F. S., K. B. McLeod, and B. Tassoulas. 2019. *A Guide on How to Insure a Natural Asset*. Arlington, VA: The Nature Conservancy.

Ferrario, F., M. W. Beck, C. D. Storlazzi, F. Micheli, C. C. Shepard, and L. Airoldi. 2014. The Effectiveness of Coral Reefs for Coastal Hazard Risk Reduction and Adaptation. *Nature Communications*. 5(3794). https://doi.org/10.1038/ncomms4794.

Flaathen, T. K. and S. R. Gislason. 2007. The Effect of Volcanic Eruptions on the Chemistry of Surface Waters: The 1991 and 2000 Eruptions of Mt. Hekla, Iceland. *Journal of Volcanology and Geothermal Research*. 164(4): pp. 293–316. https://doi.org/10.1016/j.jvolgeores.2007.05.014.

Forrester, G. E., R. L. Flynn, L. M. Forrester, and L. L. Jarecki. 2015. Episodic Disturbance from Boat Anchoring Is a Major Contributor to, but Does Not Alter the Trajectory of, Long-Term Coral Reef Decline. *PloS One*. 10(12). https://doi.org/10.1371/journal.pone.0144498.

Fox, H., J. S. Pet, R. Dahuri, and R. L. Caldwell. 2000. Coral Reef Restoration after Blast Fishing in Indonesia. *Proceedings 9th International Coral Reef Symposium* (October).

Fox, H. E., P. J. Mous, J. S. Pet, A. H. Muljadi, and R. L. Caldwell. 2005. Experimental Assessment of Coral Reef Rehabilitation Following Blast Fishing. *Conservation Biology*. 19(1): pp. 98–107. https://doi.org/10.1111/j.1523-1739.2005.00261.x.

Gedan, K. B., M. L. Kirwan, E. Wolanski, E. B. Barbier, and B. R. Sillman. 2011. The Present and Future Role of Coastal Wetland Vegetation in Protecting Shorelines: Answering Recent Challenges to the Paradigm. *Climate Change*. 106: pp. 7–29. https://doi.org/10.1007/s10584-010-0003-7.

Gillies, C., S. A. Castine, H. K. Alleway, C. Crawford, J. A. Fitzsimons, B. Hancock, P. Koch, D. McAfee, I. M. McLeod, and P. S. E. zu Emgassen. 2020. Conservation Status of the Oyster Reef Ecosystem of Southern and Eastern Australia. *Global Ecology and Conservation*. 22(June): p. e00988. https://doi.org/10.1016/j.gecco.2020.e00988.

Giri, C., E. Ochieng, L. L. Tieszen, Z. Zhu, A. Singh, T. Loveland, J. Masek, and N. Duke. 2010. Status and Distribution of Mangrove Forests of the World using Earth Observation Satellite Data. *Global Ecology and Biography*. 20(1). https://doi.org/10.1111/j.1466-8238.2010.00584.x.

Global Environment Facility (GEF). 2021. Partnerships for Coral Reef Finance and Insurance in Asia and the Pacific. https://publicpartnershipdata.azureedge.net/gef/GEFProjectVersions/1afdeffd-3504-ea11-a841-000d3a37557b_CEOEndorsement.pdf.

Goldberg, L., D. Lagomasino, N. Thomas, and T. Fatoyinbo. 2020. Global Declines in Human-Driven Mangrove Loss. *Global Change Biology*. 26(10): pp. 5844–5855. https://doi.org/10.1111/gcb.15275.

Grabowski, J. H., R. D. Brumbaugh, R. F. Conrad, A. G. Keeler, J. J. Opaluch, C. H. Peterson, M. F. Piehler, S. P. Powers, and A. R. Smyth. 2012. Economic Valuation of Ecosystem Services Provided by Oyster Reefs. *Bioscience*. 62(10): pp. 900–909. https://doi.org/10.1525/bio.2012.62.10.10.

Guest, J., A. Heyward, M. Omori, K. Iwao, A. Morse, and C. Boch. 2010. Rearing Coral Larvae for Reef Rehabilitation. In A. J. Edwards, ed. *Reef Rehabilitation Manual*. pp. 73–98. St. Lucia, Australia: The Coral Reef Targeted Research & Capacity Building for Management Program. https://eprints.ncl.ac.uk/file_store/production/162691/3DB9907B-DE8C-4FB0-979C-3D8B9C4EA719.pdf.

Guest, J. R., M. V. Baria, E. D. Gomez, A. J. Heyward, and A. J. Edwards. 2014. Closing the Circle: Is it Feasible to Rehabilitate Reefs with Sexually Propagated Corals? *Coral Reefs*. 33: pp. 45–55. https://doi.org/10.1007/s00338-013-1114-1.

Harper, S., M. Adshade, V. W. Y. Lam, D. Pauly, and U. Rashid Sumaila. 2020. Valuing Invisible Catches: Estimating the Global Contribution by Women to Small-Scale Marine Capture Fisheries Production. *PloS One*. 15(3): p. e0228912. https://doi.org/10.1371/journal.pone.0228912.

Harrison, P. L., D. W. dela Cruz, K. A. Cameron, and P. C. Cabaitan. 2021. Increased Coral Larval Supply Enhances Recruitment for Coral and Fish Habitat Restoration. *Frontiers in Marine Science.* 8(750210). https://www.frontiersin.org/articles/10.3389/fmars.2021.750210/full.

Harvell, D., E. Jordán-Dahlgren, S. Merkel, E. Rosenberg, L. Raymundo, G. Smith, E. Weil, and B. Willis. 2007. Coral Disease, Environmental Drivers, and the Balance between Coral and Microbial Associates. *Oceanography.* 20: pp. 172–195. https://researchonline.jcu.edu.au/2705/1/2705_Harvell_et_al_2007.pdf.

Hein, M., I. McLeod, E. Shaver, T. Vardi, S. Pioch, L. Boström-Einarsson, M. Ahmed, and G. Grimsditch. 2020. *Coral Reef Restoration as a Strategy to Improve Ecosystem Services— A Guide to Coral Restoration Methods.* Nairobi, Kenya: United Nations Environment Programme. https://www.icriforum.org/wp-content/uploads/2021/01/Hein-et-al.-2020_UNEP-report-1.pdf.

Hein, M. Y. and F. Staub. 2021. *Mapping the Global Funding Landscape for Coral Reef Restoration.* International Coral Reef Initiative. https://icriforum.org/wp-content/uploads/2021/11/Hein-Staub-2021-Mapping-the-Global-Funding-Landscape-for-Coral-Reef-Restoration-ICRI-WEB.pdf.

Hesp, P. A. 2008. Coastal Dunes in the Tropics and Temperate Regions: Location, Formation, Morphology, and Vegetation Processes. In L. Martinez and N. P. Psuty, eds. *Coastal Dunes: Ecology and Conservation.* pp. 29–49. New York: Springer.

Hoegh-Guldberg, O. 1999. Climate Change, Coral Bleaching and the Future of the World's Coral Reefs. *Marine and Freshwater Research.* 50: pp. 839–866. https://doi.org/10.1071/MF99078.

Hoegh-Guldberg, O., H. Hoegh-Guldberg, J. E. Veron, A. Green, E. D. Gomez, J. Lough, M. King, Ambariyanto, L. Hansen, and J. Cinner. 2009. *The Coral Triangle and Climate Change: Ecosystems, People and Societies at Risk.* Brisbane: WWF Australia. https://wwfint.awsassets.panda.org/downloads/climate_change___coral_triangle_summary_report.pdf.

Houk, P. 2011. Volcanic Disturbances and Coral Reefs. In D. Hopley, ed. *Encyclopedia of Modern Coral Reefs, Encyclopedia of Earth Sciences Series.* pp. 1138–1140. Springer Dordrecht. https://doi.org/10.1007/978-90-481-2639-2_264.

Hu, Y., B. Tian, L. Yuan, X. Li, Ying-Huang, R. Shi, X. Jiang, I. Wang, and C. Sun. 2021. Mapping Coastal Salt Marshes in China Using Time Series of Sentinel-1 SAR. *ISPRS Journal of Photogrammetry and Remote Sensing.* 173: pp. 122–134. https://doi.org/10.1016/j.isprsjprs.2021.01.003.

Hutchison, J., A. Manica, R. Swetnam, A. Balmford, and M. Spalding. 2014. Predicting Global Patterns in Mangrove Forest Biomass. *Conservation Letters.* 7(3): pp. 233–240. https://doi.org/10.1111/conl.12060.

Iyer, V., K. Mathias, D. Meyers, R. Victurine, and M. Walsh. 2018. *Finance Tools for Coral Reef Conservation: A Guide.* Wildlife Conservation Society. https://static1.squarespace.com/static/57e1f17b37c58156a98f1ee4/t/5c7d85219b747a7942c16e01/1551730017189/50+Reefs+Finance+Guide+FINAL-sm.pdf.

Jackson, J., M. Donovan, K. Cramer, and V. Lam, eds. 2014. *Status and Trends of Caribbean Coral Reefs,* pp. 1970–2012. Gland, Switzerland: Global Coral Reef Monitoring Network, IUCN.

REFERENCES

Jantzen, C. 2016. Coral Reef Restoration – Limitations, Challenges, and Opportunities. *Secore International.* 12 December. https://www.secore.org/site/newsroom/article/coral-reef-restoration-limitations-challenges-and-opportunities.149.html.

Jennings, S. and N. V. C. Polunin. 1995. Comparative Size and Composition of Yield from Six Fijian Reef Fisheries. *Journal of Fish Biology.* 46(1): pp. 28–46. https://doi.org/10.1111/j.1095-8649.1995.tb05945.x.

Kirwan, M. and J. P. Megonigal. 2013. Tidal Wetland Stability in the Face of Human Impacts and Sea-Level Rise. *Nature.* 504: pp. 53–60. https://doi.org/10.1038/nature12856.

Knoche, S., T. F. Ihde, G. Samonte, H. M. Townsend, D. Lipton, K. A. Lewis, and S. Steinback. 2020. *Estimating Ecological Benefits and Socio-Economic Impacts from Oyster Reef Restoration in the Choptank River Complex, Chesapeake Bay.* NOAA Technical Memo, NMFS-OHC-6. https://repository.library.noaa.gov/view/noaa/24759.

Kousky, C. and S. E. Light. 2019. Insuring Nature. *Duke Law Journal.* 69: pp. 323–376. https://scholarship.law.duke.edu/cgi/viewcontent.cgi?article=3996&context=dlj.

Lagomasino, D., T. Fatoyinbo, E. Castañeda-Moya, B. D. Cook, P. M. Montesano, C. S. R. Neigh, L. A. Corp, L. E. Ott, S. Chavez, and D. C. Morton. 2021. Storm Surge and Ponding Explain Mangrove Dieback in Southwest Florida following Hurricane Irma. *Nature Communications.* 12: p. 4003. https://doi.org/10.1038/s41467-021-24253-y.

Lathan and Watkins, LLP. 2020. *The Book of Jargon Environmental, Social and Governance, First Edition.* https://rg-www-prod-cd.azurewebsites.net/admin/Upload/Documents/Environmental_Social_Governance.2.pdf.

Lau, J. and C. Ruano-Chamorro. 2021. *Gender Equality in Coral Reef Socio-Ecological Systems: Literature Review.* June. https://careclimatechange.org/wp-content/uploads/2021/06/Literature-Review_Gender-Equality-and-Coral-Reefs_-15-June-2021-FINAL.pdf.

Le Bas, M. J. and A. L. Streckeisen. 1991. The IUGS Systematics of Igneous Rocks. *Journal of the Geological Society.* 148(5): pp. 825–833. https://doi.org/10.1144/gsjgs.148.5.0825.

Lowe, R. J., E. McLeod, B. G. Reguero, S. Altman, J. Harris, B. Hancock, Remment ter Hofstede, E. Randle, E. Shaver, and J. M. Smith. 2021. Chapter 12: Reefs. In T. S. Bridges, J. K. King, J. D. Simm, M. W. Beck, G. Collins, Quirijn, and R. K. Mohan, eds. *International Guidelines on Nature and Nature-Based Features for Flood Risk Management.* pp. 559–635. Vicksburg, Mississippi: US Army Corps of Engineers Research and Development Center. http://dx.doi.org/10.21079/11681/41946.

Majumdar, S. D., S. Hazra, S. Giri, A. Chanda, K. Gupta, A. Mukhopadhyay, and S. Dam Roy. 2018. Threats to Coral Reef Diversity of Andaman Islands, India: A Review. *Regional Studies in Marine Science.* 24: pp. 237–250. https://doi.org/10.1016/j.rsma.2018.08.011.

Martínez, M. I., N. P. Psuty, and R. A. Lubke. 2008. A Perspective on Coastal Dunes. In M. L. Martinez and N. P. Psuty, eds. *Coastal Dunes: Ecology and Conservation.* pp. 3–10. New York: Springer.

Martinez, N., S. Young, D. Carroll, D. Williams, J. Pollard, M. Christopher, F. Carus, D. Jones, S. Heard, and B. Franklin. 2021. *Wildfire Resilience Insurance: Quantifying the Risk Reduction of Ecological Forestry with Insurance.* The Nature Conservancy and Willis Towers Watson. https://www.nature.org/content/dam/tnc/nature/en/documents/FINALwildfireresilienceinsurance6.27.21.pdf.

Maypa, A. P., G. R. Russ, A. C. Alcala, and H. P. Calumpong. 2002. Long-Term Trends in Yield and Catch Rates of the Coral Reef Fishery at Apo Island, Central Philippines. *Marine and Freshwater Research*. 53(2): pp. 207–213. https://doi.org/10.1071/MF01134.

McIvor, A., I. Möller, T. Spencer, and M. Spalding. 2012. *Reduction of Wind and Swell Waves by Mangroves*. Cambridge Coastal Research Unit: The Nature Conservancy and Wetlands International. http://www.naturalcoastalprotection.org/documents/reduction-of-wind-and-swell-waves-by-mangroves.

Mcowen, C. J., L. V. Weatherdon, J.-W. Van Bochove, E. Sullivan, S. Blyth, C. Zockler, D. Stanwell-Smith, N. Kingston, C. S. Martin, and M. Spalding. 2017. A Global Map of Saltmarshes. *Biodiversity Data Journal*. 5: p. e11764. https://doi.org/10.3897/BDJ.5.e11764.

Meirovich, H., S. Peters, and A. R. Rios. 2013. Financial instruments and Mechanisms for Climate Change Programs in Latin America and the Caribbean, A Guide for Ministries of Finance. *Policy Brief* No. IDB-PB-212. Inter-American Development Bank, Climate Change and Sustainability Division.

Menéndez, P., I. J. Losada, M. W. Beck, S. Torres-Ortega, A. Espejo, S. Narayan, P. Díaz-Simal, and G.-M. Lange. 2018. Valuing the Protection Service of Mangroves at National Scale: The Philippines. *Ecosystem Services*. 34: pp. 24–36. https://doi.org/10.1016/j.ecoser.2018.09.005.

Menéndez, P., I. J. Losada, S. Torres-Ortega, S. Narayan, and M. W. Beck. 2020. The Global Flood Protection Benefits of Mangroves. *Scientific Reports*. 10(4404). https://doi.org/10.1038/s41598-020-61136-6.

Mesoamerican Reef Fund. 2022a. Hurricane Lisa Triggers First Pay-Out of Mesoamerican Reef Insurance Programme to Finance Immediate Reef Response in Belize. Press release. 11 November. https://marfund.org/en/hurricane-lisa-triggers-first-pay-out-of-mesoamerican-reef-insurance-programme-to-finance-immediate-reef-response-in-belize/.

———. 2022b. *Operation Guidelines for the Emergency Fund for the Mesoamerican Reef (MAR)*. Mesoamerican Reef Fund, Reef Rescue Initiative. https://fondosam.org/private/documentos-1-2/2._EmergencyFundGuidelines_MAR_Fund_RRI-May2022-ENG.pdf.

Miller, S. L., G. B. McFall, and A. W. Hulbert. 1993. *Guidelines and Recommendations for Coral Reef Restoration in the Florida Keys National Marine Sanctuary*. Wilmington, North Carolina: National Undersea Research Center, University of North Carolina at Wilmington.

Moberg, F. and C. Folke. 1999. Ecological Goods and Services of Coral Reef Ecosystems. *Ecological Economics*. 29(2): pp. 215–233. https://doi.org/10.1016/S0921-8009(99)00009-9.

Moulding, A. L., V. N. Kosmynin, and D. S. Gilliam. 2012. Coral Recruitment to Two Vessel Grounding Sites off Southeast Florida, USA. *Revista de Biología Tropical*. 60: pp. 99–108. https://www.scielo.sa.cr/scielo.php?script=sci_arttext&pid=S0034-77442012000500009.

Muir, M. 2022. Resilience Bonds: A Concept too Ambitious or Ahead of its Time? *Trading Risk*. https://www.trading-risk.com/article/29o65vrdorizfddm9bhts/resilience-bonds-a-concept-too-ambitious-or-ahead-or-its-time.

Mumby, P. J., C. P. Dahlgreen, A. R. Harborne, C. V. Kappel, F. Micheli, D. R. Brumbaugh, and K. E. Holmes. 2006. Fishing, Trophic Cascades, and the Process of Grazing on Coral Reefs. *Science*. 311(5757): pp. 98–101. https://doi.org/10.1126/science.1121129.

Muttray, M. and B. Reedijk. 2009. Design of Concrete Armour Layers. *Hansa International Maritime Journal*. 6: pp. 111–118.

Nakamura, R., W. Ando, H. Yamamoto, M. Kitano, A. Sato, M. Nakamura, H. Kayanne, and M. Omori. 2011. Corals Mass-Cultured from Eggs and Transplanted as Juveniles to their Native, Remote Coral Reef. *Marine Ecology Progress Series*. 436: pp. 161–168. https://doi.org/10.3354/meps09257.

National Academies of Sciences, Engineering, and Medicine. 2019. *A Research Review of Interventions to Increase the Persistence and Resilience of Coral Reefs*. Washington, DC: The National Academies Press. https://nap.nationalacademies.org/catalog/25279/a-research-review-of-interventions-to-increase-the-persistence-and-resilience-of-coral-reefs.

National Marine Fisheries Service. 2016. *Management Plan for Caribbean Acropora Population Enhancement*. United States: National Oceanic and Atmospheric Administration, Coral Reef Conservation Program. https://repository.library.noaa.gov/view/noaa/13515.

Newton, K., I. M. Côté, G. M. Pilling, S. Jennings, and N. K. Dulvy. 2007. Current and Future Sustainability of Island Coral Reef Fisheries. *Current Biology*. 17(7): pp. 655-658. https://doi.org/10.1016/j.cub.2007.02.054.

Okamoto, M., S. Nojima, S. Fujiwara, and Y. Furushima. 2008. Development of Ceramic Settlement Devices for Coral Reef Restoration using in situ Sexual Reproduction of Corals. *Fisheries Science*. 74(6): pp. 1245–1253. https://doi.org/10.1111/j.1444-2906.2008.01649.x.

Omori, M. 2011. Degradation and Restoration of Coral Reefs: Experience in Okinawa, Japan. *Marine Biology Research*. 7(1): pp. 3–12. https://doi.org/10.1080/17451001003642317.

Onofrietti, M. 2022. Traditional and Natural Insurance Protection Against Climate Change Hazards: Insurance Company Reactions to Climate Change. Webinar presentation, Pacific International Center for High Technology Research, 27 January. https://www.pichtr.org/climate/capacity-building/traditional-and-natural-insurance-protection-against-climate-change-hazards/.

Pandolfi, J. M., A. W. Tudhope, G. Burr, J. Chappell, E. Edinger, M. Frey, R. Steneck, C. Sharma, A. Yeates, and M. Jennions. 2006. Mass Mortality Following Disturbance in Holocene Coral Reefs from Papua New Guinea. *Geology*. 34(11): pp. 949–952. https://doi.org/10.1130/G22814A.1.

Pérez-Cervantes, E., F. P. Urrutia, L. Á. Filip, F. S. Fajardo, C. R. Alvarado, and M. A. Rocha. 2020. *Coral Reefs Damages Caused by Hurricanes in the Caribbean and their Correlation with the Characteristics of Hurricanes and Reef*. Mesoamerican Reef Rescue Initiative – MAR Fund, UNAM, and The Nature Conservancy. http://dx.doi.org/10.13140/RG.2.2.33420.18564.

Peterson, C. H., J. H. Grabowski, and S. P. Powers. 2003. Estimated Enhancement of Fish Production Resulting from Restoring Oyster Reef Habitat: Quantitative Valuation. *Marine Ecology Progress Series*. 264: pp. 249–264. https://doi.org/10.3354/meps264249.

Precht, W. F., B. E. Gintert, M. L. Robbart, R. Fura, and R. Van Woesik. 2016. Unprecedented Disease-Related Coral Mortality in Southeastern Florida. *Scientific Reports*. 6(1): pp. 1–11. https://doi.org/10.1038/srep31374.

Randall, C. J., A. P. Negri, K. M. Quigley, T. Foster, G. F. Ricardo, N. S. Webster, L. K. Bay, P. L. Harrison, R. C. Babcock, and A. J. Heyward. 2020. Sexual Production of Corals for Reef Restoration in the Anthropocene. *Marine Ecology Progress Series*. 635: pp. 203–232. https://doi.org/10.3354/meps13206.

Reef Resilience Network. 2022. Sustainable Financing. 21 December. https://reefresilience.org/management-strategies/restoration/project-planning/sustainable-financing/.

Reguero, B. G., M. W. Beck, D. Schmid, D. Stadtmüller, J. Raepple, S. Schüssele, and K. Pfliegner. 2020. Financing Coastal Resilience by Combining Nature-Based Risk Reduction with Insurance. *Ecological Economics*. 169(106487). https://doi.org/10.1016/j.ecolecon.2019.106487.

Reliefweb. 2019. *Asia Pacific Regional Hazard Map: Last 50 Years Tropical Storms in Asia-Pacific: 1968–2018*. https://reliefweb.int/map/world/asia-pacific-regional-hazard-map-last-50-years-tropical-storms-asia-pacific-1968-2018 (last modified 19 March 2019).

Reopanichkul, P., T. A. Schlacher, R. W. Carter, and S. Worachananant. 2009. Sewage Impacts Coral Reefs at Multiple Levels of Ecological Organization. *Marine Pollution Bulletin*. 58(9): pp. 1356–1362. https://doi.org/10.1016/j.marpolbul.2009.04.024.

Roa-Quiaoit, H. A. 2021. *ADB Coral Reef Insurance: Synthesis El Nido-Coron*. Manila.

Rodriguez, A. B., F. J. Fodrie, J. T. Ridge, N. L. Lindquist, E. J. Theuerkauf, S. E. Coleman, J. H. Grabowski, M. C. Brodeur, R. K. Gittman, and D. A. Keller. 2014. Oyster Reefs can Outpace Sea-Level Rise. *Nature Climate Change*. 2: pp. 493–497. https://doi.org/10.1038/nclimate2216.

Rogers, M., F. S. Fajardo, L. Geselbracht, M. Musgrove, E. Roberts, and J. Schmidt. 2022. *Relevance and Feasibility of Mangrove Insurance in Mexico, Florida, and The Bahamas*. Arlington, VA: The Nature Conservancy.

Saintilan, N., N. S. Khan, E. Ashe, J. J. Kelleway, K. Rogers, C. D. Woodroffe, and B. P. Horton. 2020. Thresholds for Mangrove Survival under Rapid Sea Level Rise. *Science*. 368(6495): pp. 1118–1121. https://doi.org/10.1126/science.aba2656.

Shafir, S., J. Van Rijn, and B. Rinkevich. 2006. Steps in the Construction of Underwater Coral Nursery, an Essential Component in Reef Restoration Acts. *Marine Biology*. 149(3): pp. 679–687. https://doi.org/10.1007/s00227-005-0236-6.

Shaver, E. C., E. McLeod, M. Y. Hein, S. R. Palumbi, K. Quigley, T. Vardi, and P. J. Mumby. 2022. A Roadmap to Integrating Resilience into the Practice of Coral Reef Restoration. *Global Change Biology*. https://doi.org/10.1111/gcb.16212.

Smith, D. 2022. Mars Assisted Reef Restoration System. International Coral Reef Initiative. 21 December. https://icriforum.org/mars-assisted-reef-restoration-system/.

Spalding, M. 2010. *World Atlas of Mangroves*. London, UK: Routledge. https://doi.org/10.4324/9781849776608.

Spalding, M., R. D. Brumbaugh, and E. Landis. 2016. *Atlas of Ocean Wealth*. Arlington, Virginia: The Nature Conservancy. https://www.researchgate.net/publication/303984281_Atlas_of_Ocean_Wealth.

Spalding, M., L. Burke, S. A. Wood, J. Ashpole, J. Hutchison, and P. Z. Ermgassen. 2017. Mapping the Global Value and Distribution of Coral Reef Tourism. *Marine Policy*. 82: pp. 104–113. https://doi.org/10.1016/j.marpol.2017.05.014.

Spalding, M., M. Kainuma, and L. Collins. 2010. *World Atlas of Mangroves (version 3.1)*. London, UK: Earthscan, London. https://doi.org/10.34892/w2ew-m835.

Spergel, B. and M. Moye. 2004. *Financing Marine Conservation*. Washington, DC: World Wildlife Fund. https://wwfeu.awsassets.panda.org/downloads/fmcnewfinal.pdf.

Teh, L. S. L., L. C. L. Teh, and U. Rashid Sumaila. 2013. A Global Estimate of the Number of Coral Reef Fishers. *PLOS One*. 8(6). https://doi.org/10.1371/journal.pone.0065397.

The Lab. Restoration Insurance Service Company. https://www.climatefinancelab.org/project/coastal-risk-reduction/ (accessed 22 December 2022).

The Nature Conservancy (TNC). 2021a. *A Reef Insurance Primer: Hurricane Damages to Reefs, Repair and Restoration Options and Costs*. Arlington, VA: The Nature Conservancy. https://www.nature.org/content/dam/tnc/nature/en/documents/Reef_insurance_primer.pdf.

———. 2021b. *Nature's Remedy: Improving Flood Resilience through Community Insurance and Nature-Based Mitigation*. Munich RE and The Nature Conservancy. https://www.nature.org/content/dam/tnc/nature/en/documents/ImprovingFloodResilienceThroughInsuranceandNatureBasedMitigation_21NOV01.pdf.

———. 2021c. The Government of Belize Partners with The Nature Conservancy to Conserve 30% of its Ocean Through Debt Conversion. Press release. 5 November. https://www.nature.org/en-us/newsroom/blue-bonds-belize-conserve-thirty-percent-of-ocean-through-debt-conversion/.

———. 2022. The Nature Conservancy Announces First-Ever Coral Reef Insurance Policy in the U.S. Press release. 21 November. https://www.nature.org/en-us/newsroom/first-ever-us-coral-reef-insurance-policy/.

Torell, E., J. Castro, A. Lazarte, and D. Bilecki. 2021. Analysis of Gender Roles in Philippine Fishing Communities. *Journal of International Development*. 33(1): pp. 233–255. https://doi.org/10.1002/jid.3520.

Tuivuniwai, M. 2021. *Pacific Islands Regional Oceanscape Program Synthesis Report: Sustainable Financing of the Conservation of Critical Fishery Habitats*. Pacific Islands Forum Fisheries Agency and Pacific Regional Oceanscape Program. https://www.ffa.int/system/files/PROP%20Pacific%20Ocean%20Finance%20Synthesis%20%20Report-3%20%281%29.pdf.

Turner, N. R. and D. Abigail Renegar. 2017. Petroleum Hydrocarbon Toxicity to Corals: A Review. *Marine Pollution Bulletin*. 119(1): pp. 1–16. https://doi.org/10.1016/j.marpolbul.2017.04.050.

United Nations. 2022. Latest Ocean Data. https://www.un.org/en/conferences/ocean2022/facts-figures (accessed 4 September 2022).

United Nations Climate Change. 2016. Bilateral and Multilateral Funding. https://cop23.unfccc.int/topics/climate-finance/resources/multilateral-and-bilateral-funding-sources.

United Nations Environment Programme and Global Programme of Action (UNEP/GPA). 2006. *The State of the Marine Environment: Trends and Processes*. The Hague: Coordination Office of the Global Programme of Action for the Protection of the Marine Environment from Land-Based Activities of the United Nations Environment Programme.

United Nations Environment Programme, International Sustainability Unit, International Coral Reef Initiative, and Trucost. 2018. *The Coral Reef Economy: The Business Case for Investment in the Protection, Preservation and Enhancement of Coral Reef Health*. https://wedocs.unep.org/20.500.11822/26694.

Vega Thurber, R. L., D. E. Burkepile, C. Fuchs, A. A. Shantz, R. McMinds, and J. R. Zaneveld. 2014. Chronic Nutrient Enrichment Increases Prevalence and Severity of Coral Disease and Bleaching. *Global Change Biology*. 20(2): pp. 544–554. https://doi.org/10.1111/gcb.12450.

Veron, J. E. N., O. Hoegh-Guldberg, T. M. Lenton, J. M. Lough, D. O. Obura, P. A. U. L. Pearce-Kelly, C. R. C. Sheppard, M. Spalding, M. G. Stafford-Smith, and A. D. Rogers. 2009. The Coral Reef Crisis: The Critical Importance of <350 ppm CO_2. *Marine Pollution Bulletin*. 58(10): pp. 1428–1436. https://doi.org/10.1016/j.marpolbul.2009.09.009.

Victurine, R., D. Meyers, J. Bohorquez, S. Box, J. Blythe, M. Callow, S. Jupiter, K. Schweigart, M. Walsh, and T. Bieri. 2022. *Conservation Finance for Coral Reefs*. Vibrant Oceans Initiative. https://c532f75abb9c1c021b8c-e46e473f8aadb72cf2a8ea564b4e6a76.ssl.cf5.rackcdn.com/2022/03/03/9abgqfkz8l_3.3.22_Sustainable_Finance_Whitepaper.pdf.

Ward, R., D. A. Friess, R. H. Day, and R. A. Mackenzie. 2016. Impacts of Climate Change on Mangrove Ecosystems: A Region by Region Approach. *Ecosystem Health and Sustainability*. 2(4). https://doi.org/10.1002/ehs2.1211.

Weis, J. S., K. E. A. Segarra, and P. Bernal. 2016. Salt Marshes. In *The First Global Integrated Marine Assessment: World Ocean Assessment I*. Chapter 49. Cambridge, UK: Cambridge University Press/United Nations. https://www.un.org/depts/los/global_reporting/WOA_RPROC/Chapter_49.pdf.

Wharton, J. 2021. *The Mesoamerican Reef: A Cornerstone of Sustainable Development*. Willis Towers Watson. https://marfund.org/en/wp-content/uploads/2021/10/Brief_-MAR-Insurance-Programme-_QA.pdf.

Williams, S. L., C. Sur, N. Janetski, J. A. Hollarsmith, S. Rapi, L. Barron, and S. J. Heatwole. 2019. Large-Scale Coral Reef Rehabilitation after Blast Fishing in Indonesia. *Restoration Ecology*. 27(2): pp. 447–456. https://doi.org/10.1111/rec.12866.

Willis Towers Watson. 2021. Willis Towers Watson Designs "World-First" Parametric Solution to Help Build Resilience of Sovereign Borrowers to Climate Shocks. Press release. 20 December. https://www.wtwco.com/en-SE/News/2021/12/wtw-designs-world-first-parametric-solution-to-help-build-resilience-of-sovereign-borrowers.

―――. 2023. WTW Announces Third Renewal and Expansion of Coral Reef Insurance Programme. Press release. 1 June. https://www.wtwco.com/en-us/news/2023/06/wtw-announces-third-renewal-and-expansion-of-coral-reef-insurance-programme.

Willis Towers Watson and MAR Fund. 2019. *Beneficiaries of Rapid Response Reef Risk Financing in the MAR Region*. InsuResilience Solutions Fund. https://marfund.org/en/wp-content/uploads/2020/02/Beneficiaries-of-Rapid-Response-Reef-Risk-Financing-in-the-MAR-Region.pdf.

World Bank. 2012. *Advancing Disaster Risk Financing and Insurance in ASEAN Member States: Framework and Options for Implementation*. Washington, DC: World Bank. https://openknowledge.worldbank.org/bitstream/handle/10986/12627/714530v10ESW0W00ASEAN0REPORT0June12.pdf?sequence=1&isAllowed=y.

———. 2016. *Managing Coasts with Natural Solutions: Guidelines for Measuring and Valuing the Coastal Protection Services of Mangroves and Coral Reefs*. Edited by M. W. Beck and G-M Lange. WAVES Technical Report. Washington, DC: World Bank. https://documents1.worldbank.org/curated/en/995341467995379786/pdf/Managing-coasts-with-natural-solutions-guidelines-for-measuring-and-valuing-the-coastal-protection-services-of-mangroves-and-coral-reefs.pdf.

Yayasan Konservasi Alam Nustantara (YKAN). 2021. *Indonesia Baseline Assessment Report on PPP for Coral Reef Insurance*. 21 May. Manila: Asian Development Bank.

Young, C. N., S. A. Schopmeyer, and D. Lirman. 2012. A Review of Reef Restoration and Coral Propagation Using the Threatened Genus Acropora in the Caribbean and Western Atlantic. *Bulletin of Marine Science*. 88(4): pp. 1075–1098. https://doi.org/10.5343/bms.2011.1143.

Young, S. and J. Wharton. 2020. *Pacific Ocean Finance Program—Insurance Final Report*. Willis Towers Watson. https://opocbluepacific.org/download/64/ocean-finance-mechanisms/801/analysis-and-development-of-pacific-ocean-risk-insurance.pdf.

Zepeda, C., E. McLeod, I. M. Tapia, R. R. Martinez, L. A. Filip, A. T. Banaszak, M. E. Castillo, R. S. Casarín, E. M. Baldwin, and M. Beck. 2018. *Guidance Document for Reef Management and Restoration to Improve Coastal Protection: Recommendations for Global Applications based on lessons learned in Mexico*. Mexico: The Nature Conservancy. https://media.coastalresilience.org/MAR/Guidance%20document%20for%20reef%20management%20and%20restoration%20to%20improve%20coastal%20protection.pdf.

Zepeda, C., A. C. P. Souza, J. C. H. Baca, M. M. Constantino, E. Shaver, G. G. N. Martínez, and M. Á. G. Salgado. 2019. *Early Warnings and Rapid Response Protocol: Actions to Mitigate the Impact of Tropical Cyclones on Coral Reefs*. Mexico: The Nature Conservancy. https://www.icriforum.org/wp-content/uploads/2020/12/Post-storm-protocol.pdf.